MW01031012

# I Love an Alcoholic, but Hated The Drinking

*11 Essential Strategies to*
*Survive Codependency*
*and Live in Recovery with Self-Love*

## Grace W. Wroldson

www.GraceWroldson.com

USA

ISBN-13: 978-1724459060
ISBN-10: 1724459066

Cover design by Oliviaprodesign on Fiverr.com
Formatting by Bqureshi on Fiverr.com

Published 2018
Contact: www.GraceWroldson.com

*For my child,*
*And all the children of this dilemma*

# DISCLAIMER:

This is written in a pen name to protect all involved. I do not name the alcoholic, nor myself. I also do not give advice. These are my strategies which you may use as suggestions for yourself —*if* they are right for you. And *if* you feel ready.

I am not a mental health expert nor a professional therapist. I do not (and I am unable to) offer crisis support as a writer, author, or life coach. Any perceived slight of any individual or organization is unintentional. Neither the author nor the publisher assumes any responsibility for errors, omissions, or contrary interpretations of the subject matter herein. Here, I offer my strategies with personal stories attached so that you might learn how I learned my lessons and read how I won my wisdom.

If you need urgent or immediate support for your situation, please find your local crisis center/shelter, domestic violence agency, counselor, therapist, lawyer, and/or police. Due to the sometimes physically abusive nature of alcoholism, I ask my readers to use caution, be smart, and stay safe. I had to be very resourceful, seek local help, practice safety, use authorities, and hire a lawyer. I also had to use good judgement. Please take what you like and leave the rest.

My recovery that I refer to is my own blend of various self-help programs, healing modalities and spirituality. I often refer to "the program" and "my recovery" as my own experience of using the Al-Anon Twelve-Step Family Groups, for friends and family of alcoholics.

My #1 suggestion
To get a better understanding of my story and these strategies, you may want to read *So You Love an... Alcoholic? : Lessons for a Codependent* —

first. Reading my first book of 25+ powerful lessons may help you understand how these survival strategies originated.

Also, I encourage that you and your "safe people" (people you trust, who know your circumstances, and are supportive) come up with your own strategies for your own unique situation. These were mine and some of these may help to you. Please consider crafting and creating your own survival strategies as you read along. I would love to hear from you if you would like to share any of your own brilliant survival strategies with me.

❖ Visit me at www.GraceWroldson.com

# Table of Contents

## Layer I

## Layer II

## Layer III

## Layer IV

## Bonus # 1

## Bonus # 2

# *My Prayer*

*I pray for the alcoholic,*

*I pray for those suffering from codependency,*

*I pray for the children.*

# My Serenity Prayer Version

*(After years of repeating the good old Serenity Prayer,*
*I ended up adjusting it to fit my circumstances.*
*This version came from within.)*

"God, grant me the strength to do what needs to get done.
The courage to face myself afterwards.
(with all my insane self-doubt)
And the wisdom to know what the hell
is *REALLY* going on in my life!"

— *Grace W. Wroldson*

*A special thanks to my kick-ass sponsor for "kicking" my ass*

*In loving memory of Laura.*

A woman who loved an alcoholic and lost her life.

# A Tribute to the Lois Wilson Co-Founder of Al-Anon

*"Behind every great man is an extraordinary woman,*
*in extraordinary circumstances."*
— *Grace W. Wroldson*

### *A Great Woman*

**What About Lois?**

The expression, "behind every great man is a great woman," originated sometime in the first half of the twentieth century. People often use it to try to give recognition to the wives or mothers of successful men. This is because the women often helped the men in their lives (a lot - I will add). However, women's work and contribution was unrecognized and still is unrecognized to this day. The saying gives credit to these underappreciated women. I believe Lois Wilson was a great woman who deserves recognition. The history of loving an alcoholic is important.

"What about the other victims of alcoholism?" I wondered. What about those who lived through it and survived?

**A Visit to Two Historical Sites**

I stood at Lois' grave and I sat in Lois' bedroom. At her home, now called Stepping Stones, which she shared with her husband Bill Wilson, in Bedford Hills, New York, I looked around her desk searching for clues. I went on these annual "recovery pilgrimages" where Lois and Bill walked the earth to find truth while I dealt with my alcoholic love dilemma. I wondered what Lois would say, if I could talk to her directly. I wanted to survive the disease of alcoholism with the man I loved. After all, she had survived.

Lois was the wife of a very famous alcoholic —THE Bill Wilson. He and another alcoholic, co-founded Alcoholics Anonymous (AA). Similarly, Lois and another wife co-founded Al-Anon, a Twelve-Step program for friends and family of alcoholics. I found Al-Anon but my alcoholic never found his AA. What would Lois say?

## Lois' Grave

As I took these spiritual recovery pilgrimages I pondered the history of the dilemma of an alcoholic marriage. I was connecting to my roots of recovery to its origins. I often visited the Wilson House in East Dorset, Vermont, enjoying its antique feel. One Sunday, on one of Al-Anon's yearly Pioneer Day, I stood at Lois' grave and thought about her incredible life. Buried next to her husband Bill W., an alcoholic, who was now a celebrated hero, I contemplated what it must have been like for her to be a witness to sobriety, recovery, and his primary purpose of carrying the message to other alcoholics (and thus serving others with his life). Lois's grave had only a few tokens of gratitude, while Bill's gravestone was adorned with many AA anniversary coins. I couldn't help but notice how many people visited and showed their appreciation to Bill, compared to Lois. If he was the president, Lois would have been the First Lady during the founding years of the Twelve-Step Groups. "What about Lois?" something in me stirred and asked.

I recognized how their accomplishments were appreciated differently. And something about it disturbed me. It touched that unrecognized place inside of me. Bill was very accomplished with AA, but what about Lois' achievements? She had a front row seat (or, perhaps, I'll say a side seat) to the whole alcoholic show. Fortunately for her the show turned into a sober show and she experienced some sanity and serenity with Bill's sobriety. And this is what I would call success.

I Love an Alcoholic, but Hated The Drinking

On that day, with a key in my hand, I headed to the historical Griffith House, now a small library containing several artifacts of the history of AA. I wondered why I had to work on my recovery program so much harder than most of the other Al-Anoners that I knew. It seemed like my recovery was as precious as AA was to a newly recovering alcoholic. It was then that I realized I had to work the Twelve-Steps like my life depended on it because the alcoholic that I loved never reached sobriety or recovery. I would not be buried next to him (with the same last name) like Lois and Bill. So, I had to do all the heavy lifting of working the Twelve-Step "sister program" of Al-Anon myself. I could not rely on my partner's AA recovery to carry us both to a sober, sane, and serene life because he never found it. I had to. And, so, I did.

## Bill's Childhood Bedroom

Part of that day, I found myself sitting in Bill Wilson's childhood bedroom. I thought about the history of alcoholism and the history of recovery with the Twelve-Steps and how it all started with one man willing share his mistakes, pain, and problems. But as a cofounder of AA, Bill had a wife who was part of his transformation too. What about her? How did she play a role in his success and sobriety? I often thought about her struggle, the challenges, and the changes she had to go through being married to an alcoholic. How much did she sacrifice to be married to him? How much did she sacrifice to stay married to an alcoholic and see the AA program evolve? During my research, I uncovered that she was unable to have children and couldn't adopt children due to factors such as Bill's previous "drinking years." That surely was a big sacrifice.

## Al-Anon's Beginnings

Thankfully, Lois started Al-Anon to help women like me and thankfully, I found it. Sometimes a scary thought would cross my mind —what if Bill didn't co-found the Twelve-Step Program of AA? Would alcoholism have continued wrecking relationships and entire lives with no solution? Where would I be? It was a scary thought that made me immediately grateful.

I am grateful for Lois because I found relief, healing, courage, and growth in Al-Anon. After twenty years in the Al-Anon program, not just surviving but now thriving, I became grateful to the alcoholic for he brought me into my own program of recovery. Being grateful for the alcoholic was another turning point in the progress of my recovery.

## My Solo Recovery

Stepping on the white marble stones that lead to the Griffith House, walking alone, I had a miraculous mental shift in my perception. My anger with the alcoholic for not entering AA dissolved and turned into gratitude. I realized that I was grateful (to myself) for having had the courage to work my recovery program and not rely on a man or a marriage to do it for me. Finding my own ways to survive the disease of alcoholism, working recovery for myself, made my recovery for me. So, all my hard-work was not mistakenly dedicated to keeping a relationship — it was for me. And my story is a testimony to self-love.

I experienced the promises of AA while working and staying in the Al-Anon program for myself. I sat in this historical place — a place of power where I imagined that I was connecting to the roots of my recovery, where it all began. It began when Bill was a little boy. And with a great love, Lois loved that little boy. Her love was in my recovery. I could feel it.

## The Original Manuscript of AA

In the small library of the historical site, I began reading the original manuscript of AA, (copied in high definition). It felt like I was reading an ancient historical artifact that I could decode (only because I had been in recovery long enough to learn the language of the program). In a state of awe, I wanted to kneel down and bow before it in some type of ceremonial sacred act. Others have spent ten, twenty, or even thirty years growing in Twelve-Step recovery rooms might be able to relate to my feeling. This was the original text that saved my life, gave me solutions, steps, and hope.

## My Original Manuscript of *So You Love an... Alcoholic?*

It was also a moment of relief because at that time I was still struggling with the manuscript for my first book. To my relief, I discovered that the AA manuscript needed the same type of editing that my first book required. At first, I, too, wrote entirely in "you-statements" (second person). Then, painstakingly, for moral and legal reasons, I had to go back and replace all the you's with "I's". It was interesting to see that Bill's efforts at his first manuscript of Alcoholics Anonymous, was corrected (marked in pencil and red ink) to replace all the you's with we's. I realized then that when a Higher Power speaks to us, it comes in as very personal. I found it quite intriguing to notice that a Higher Power seems to speak in "you-statements."

It was overwhelming to completely rewrite my entire first manuscript to "I-statements" making it all first person. It took a long and laborious seven years of correcting and editing. It was then that I understood that the words of a Higher Power and the words from our soul are meant for us, and then we can carry the message to others. I realized translation was required. Decoding is required. So, please translate and decode this book for yourself according to how it may fit into your personal journey.

## Lois Didn't Just Play a Supporting Role — She Played a Main Role

To learn more about this woman, I watched the movie based on her life, *When Love Is Not Enough: The Lois Wilson Story*. It's based on the true story of the enduring but troubled love between Lois and Bill. Watching the relationship dynamic portrayed, I noticed that Lois had her own brilliance and did play more than just a supporting role. In the movie she pointed out to Bill that when he helped another alcoholic he was helped. That in itself was a crucial observance. We can't see our own blind spots. We also sometimes cannot see ourselves while we are going through something. We need supportive people. We are too in "it" to see clearly. We also can't see when we are under the influence or impaired by alcohol or battling an addiction. Thankfully, Lois was watching, and she made constructive critical comments to Bill. Thankfully, someone was sober.

## The Flying Shoe

As I watched the movie, I noted that before AA and before sobriety, Bill was becoming a legendary money-maker. Lois supported Bill's efforts to meet with Wall Street companies and make his big money. Seems to me that she was always looking out for him by pointing out key successful tips he followed up on. Did anyone else catch that? Is anyone else seeing the importance of Lois' role in Bill's successes? This tells me that Lois was a big part of the success of AA (maybe more than we all realize). She lived to be 97 years old. On her obituary, it reads: "she was revered as "the first lady of Al-Anon," and as a living reminder of the beginnings five decades ago of the Alcoholics Anonymous self-help movement."

The part of the movie that spoke the loudest to me was the dramatic moment when the actress playing Lois, Winona Ryder, took off her shoe and threw it at Bill. She was crying and yelling at the same time. She was asking the question I believe all of us ask when the disease of alcoholism has taken over the person we love and there is nothing left for us. What about us we wonder? When will it be our turn to be loved? When we will come first?

To me, Lois Wilson was one of the most important women in the twentieth century. Her life blessed the entire alcoholic-loving-world. By being a co-survivor of the disease of alcoholism, she contributed to my recovery and maybe to yours, too, if you are in a Twelve-Step program. I give thanks to this amazing woman that I will never get to personally meet. Her sacrifices led to my salvation. She is a woman who knew about the struggles of loving an alcoholic. And she would have known about me. She was a woman who loved.

*"Hearts understand in ways minds cannot."*
— *Lois Wilson*

**So I ask those of us caught up in loving an alcoholic,**

> ➤ **What about Lois?**
> ➤ **What about us?**
> ➤ **And What about you?**

# *Step One*

## *(my version)*

*I admitted I was powerless over people, places, and things (including alcohol, the alcoholic, my codependency) and thus my life had become unmanageable.*

*—Step One -- adapted from The Twelve Steps of Alcoholics Anonymous, adopted by Al-Anon, a Twelve Step support group for friends and families of alcoholics, then modified by me*

# Does the Drinking Bother You?

My sponsor told me to ask myself (and answer) one simple question, "Does the drinking bother you?"

*The Drinking*
*The drinker would say to me,*
*"I don't have a problem drinking,*
**you** *just have a problem with my drinking."*
*— Anonymous Alcoholic*

He was right. Yes, I did! The drinker was masterful at deflection, distraction, and redirection. He did anything and everything to be able to continue to drink. He dodged my nagging interference. The truth was I was getting in his way. When he was given the choice between me or the drink, he always chose the drink. When given the choice between the drink or our child (and having a family with me), he still chose the drink. My ultimatums didn't stop his drinking. What the hell was he thinking?

## Was he an alcoholic?

After the initial ten years I spent in Al-Anon, a Twelve-Step recovery program for friends and family of alcoholics, I will admit I wasn't entirely sure if he was an alcoholic. All I knew was he liked to drink, and his drinking bothered the heck out of me. But I also knew that Al-Anon was the right place for me. I was advised that I couldn't call him an alcoholic unless he called himself that. Ha! In my case, with my drinker, I saw no chance of that ever happening.

So, I had to decide once and for all was his drinking just normal, casual, social drinking or was it more. As a spectator watching his drinking sport, it was more than normal (way more). To me, his drinking was abnormal which was why I was growing more and more uncomfortable with it. The bottom line was this: his drinking bothered me.

His drinking was every day. The one time that I had convinced him to go to couples counseling with me to save our relationship in our early twenties, the counselor asked him an important question:

"How much do you drink?" she asked him directly.

I was surprised, first by her boldness, then by his answer. I was on the edge of my seat.

He asked, "Daily?"

"Sure, " she replied.

"A six-pack a day," he said honestly.

I was shocked. Wait. I know I saw him with a beer daily, but I wasn't counting. Actually, I lost count a long time ago when I went into denial.

Then the counselor turned to me and asked me if that was OK with me. "No," I said. And then there was silence.

On the way out of the session, the drinker told me that this will be the first and the last time he would ever attend a therapy session with me. And, sadly, I can tell you that he kept his word. Yet, I proceeded to stay in that relationship for fifteen long years watching him drink. Was he an alcoholic? I can't say for sure because I learned that it is usually a self-diagnosed disease. Do *I* think he had a problem with alcohol? Yes. Will he admit that? No. So, where do we stand?

For the purposes of cutting through the bullshit and getting clear on the problem I was dealing with - the drinker and his drinking - I began to call him an alcoholic. It felt wrong to just keep saying "the drinker in my life." I did an important thing by labeling my situation more accurately, I got clear. I became really clear that I was in an alcoholic relationship and like him, was also being affected by the disease of alcoholism. By naming it, I was able to seek help. Of course, he wouldn't admit to a problem with his drinking. He didn't want to give it up. And to this day, he hasn't.

**What is more important?**

What's more important is that I didn't give up on myself. I got sober from the dysfunctional relationship of enabling, codependency, and my addiction to loving him regardless. I moved on and became free of my codependent ways. I found a program of recovery - for me. I became happy without him and his marriage to his drinking. I broke my addiction to loving him and was able to live a more fulfilling life without him. That's what mattered. Thankfully, I didn't marry him. I married a new version of me. I broke my heart to successfully leave him and then I held onto my heart. I got away from the drinking, the alcoholic, and so did my child.

So, yes, the drinking bothered me. Yes, I did have a problem with his drinking. That included how much drinking he was doing and the drinking and driving. However, I learned to focus on my thinking which was more bothersome because I was still hanging onto the drinker. I had enough proof that drinking destroys and I didn't want to be destroyed.

I stopped asking, "What the hell is he thinking?" And I started asking, "What the hell was I thinking?" Did my thinking bother me? Yes.

# Welcome to My Survival Strategies

*"Love is the ultimate law of life."*
*— message from a Yogi tea bag*
*(I wondered...who said this? And did they love an alcoholic?)*

*"All serious daring starts from within."*
*— Eudora Welty, On Writing*

## Are You Unhappy?

Can you imagine what it would be like to wake up without the bitterness?

I finally stopped "relationshiping" long enough to ask myself, "Hey, wait, am I happy?"

Yes, I loved an alcoholic. Yes, I loved an alcoholic who had fifteen years of continuous drinking. But, no, I was not happy. There was no question that I loved him, but I questioned whether I was truly loving myself. I had to go within and ask myself this question:

"What could happen for me if I loved myself?"

"Could I be happy by myself?"

I discovered my biggest survival strategy to be the "self-love solution." I found that it was able to sustain my happiness.

## A Library of Lessons Available

In my first book, *So You Love an... Alcoholic?: Lessons for a Codependent*, I claimed all of my lessons as part of my healing process. These survival strategies stemmed from those lessons for living life beyond the confines of codependency. I lived a better life after loving an active alcoholic and learned to love myself instead. If you are seeking a place to start towards happiness, I suggest reading all of those 25+ lessons in my first book of self-help secrets.

## Self-help Solutions

Sometimes the only help is self-help. I had to find the right help for me. I learned to act in my own best interest. I practiced the Al-Anon Twelve Steps, for friends and family of alcoholics, like my life depended on it. Because it did (and still does). The reward I received was not his sobriety. The gift I got was myself back. The reward was my own sobriety from codependency and freedom. And sober living from codependency is my full-time job.

Back when our alcoholic-codependent relationship was failing, I silently declared to the alcoholic in my life, "That's it! If you are not going to change —I WILL!" With that determination, and a focus on the right person (me), I took charge of my life. I stopped handing my happiness over to the alcoholic. Is it time to take back your life?

Before recovery, I was behaving like a codependent and was truly, madly, deeply, addicted to loving him. I would wake up in the morning wondering how he was feeling and not how I was feeling. Do you wake up in the morning wondering how he is feeling and not how you are feeling? Is your focus on the alcoholic and not you?

## It's Okay to Love The Alcoholic

After writing my first book, I realized that it's okay to love an alcoholic (as long as I am loving myself, too!) Sometimes, this can be done within the relationship, but for me I had to do my loving of him from a distance outside of the relationship. The most loving thing I could do for myself was to leave. The second most loving thing I could do was remain gone. I had to detach and stay separate to stay sane. It was self-loving.

Grace W. Wroldson

## How This Book Came About

I wrote for myself. At the time I was loving someone else and not loving myself, so I journaled my journey to self-love. I took a risk and opened myself up to criticism from "real" authors and writers, but I didn't care. I wanted to share my message and save as many women and children as I could with my story. May you be helped and saved.

As much as these 11 strategies are my strategies for survival, they also are stepping stones towards happiness. I had to learn to crawl before I could learn to walk, so to speak. Happiness didn't just happen overnight. I had to implement these strategies. I didn't have happiness with the heartbreak of leaving him. Truthfully, I didn't have happiness for the first couple of years —but I did have relief.

## I Lived And You Can Too!

I didn't die from the disease of alcoholism. I didn't die from the disease of codependency and loneliness. I didn't die from love-addiction, although it was close! (I saw those possibilities as very real when Laura passed away.) After fifteen years of being in an alcoholic relationship, I had completely shed my naivete that codependency doesn't kill only alcoholism does. Tragically, I watched a friend die from codependency. This is why I call this an alcoholic relationship because it's an alcoholic-codependent issue. Sadly, I also watched others die slow soul deaths without recovery. I learned that codependency was part of the disease of alcoholism and I wanted to survive. So, I worked my recovery and lived.

## What and Where Was My Happiness?

For years, I thought my happiness would come if he would just stop drinking. I also didn't realize how unhappy I was until I was out from under the relationship (and left him). My sponsor once said, "Sometimes, we need to find out what happiness is before we find out that we are unhappy." My sponsor explained that we can be in a relationship for so long that we mistakenly think that this must be all there is. Our view can be narrow and short-sighted. I found that sometimes the unhappiness that is right in front of us is all we can see, especially when we are "in" it. It still perplexes me. How could I not see how unhappy I was?

After finally leaving the alcoholic and being a few different relationships with non-alcoholics, I learned that happiness can happen for me and discovered what it looks like. My danger? I found my danger to be not continuing to work my recovery in a program despite getting out of an abusive relationship with an alcoholic. Out of recovery, I fell asleep to what was happening within and repeated my needy patterns. I would inadvertently lead myself down destructive paths with other relationships. So, who was the cause of my unhappiness? Me or the alcoholic? Sometimes, falling asleep (not staying awake with my program) meant that I got back into the same relationship with the same alcoholic. So scary!

What was my bottom line? I wanted to be loved and happy. I had to start with loving myself.

Then, I needed to ask myself this powerful question, "Am I worth it?"

After spending half of my life loving an alcoholic and not loving myself, I answered,

"Yes. Yes, I am."

And poof! My bitterness was gone!

**Questions to ask yourself:**

> ➢ Are you sick and tired of being sick and tired?
> ➢ Are you bitter from being bitter?
> ➢ Do you want to be happy?

> ❖ If you would like to read some of my other survival strategies and read FREE excerpts of my other books, please visit my website at: www.GraceWroldson.com

# My Secrets for Success,
# My Strategies

- Claiming the Lessons
- My Library of Lessons

## *X-Ray Vision*

**Dear Reader,**

This is not advice, but rather my hard-earned wisdom. What I will be sharing with you are my secrets for success. This book contains my lessons that transformed into survival strategies for loving or leaving an active alcoholic and recovering from my own codependency. I remember the moment when my lessons turned to successful life strategies —it was the same moment that I realized I had survived the alcoholic-codependent relationship.

These strategies are insights into my once codependently wired brain. Think of it like having an X-Ray of my mind, so that you can see (for yourself) how I rewired my brain with the truth.

**Inside My Newly Renovated Mind**

This private viewing into my mind will help you see the new neural pathways that my self-help strategies and recovery in Al-Anon created. I documented these strategies as I was coming out of my codependency issues and into my life of freedom from an alcoholic relationship. I began cataloguing and making a library of lessons (and strategies) for other women who wanted to find a self-help resource to this particular problem. I was creating my own encyclopedia for you and at some point I had to stop and simplify them. There are many more strategies I used, and maybe you have some of your own. Please share!

**My Story of Survival with Recovery**

After surviving a relationship with an alcoholic, I realized how incredibly difficult it was to break free. I was motivated to share some of my secrets for success because I saw how children became involved in the alcoholic-codependent drama. After my "codependent spell" cleared, I was smart enough to not just say "I learned a lesson," but also label the lesson. I wrote them down as I learned. I continued to practice recovery in Twelve-Step Groups, especially Al-Anon for friends and family of alcoholics. My recovery reached new layers and levels. In those meetings, I found other people suffering from the same torment. I saw how other women saved their lives using the program of recovery. When I was ready, I had to launch my own self-saving program which included several other types of self-help sources and an amazing sponsor with 30+ years of their own recovery work in Al-Anon.

**Writing to Remember**

I permanently nailed down the lessons, so that they might never be forgotten (by me). In writing my first book, I created a bulletin board for public reference and display. I compiled them so that they might be recalled, revisited, reinvented, and refreshed. If each were considered an isle there would be an isle of codependency, an isle of recovery, and an isle of forgiveness. To this day I reread my lessons and learned something new about myself every time! How is that?

### My Lesson:

✓ **Claim the Lessons**
✓ **As Part of my Healing Process**

There is a popular saying, "If you can't name it, you can't claim it!" I couldn't name what was happening to me before writing. As I was writing what I was learning, I also became the writer of my new life story. You can too! These lessons (which turned into strategies) are what I wanted to teach myself and finally learn. These strategies are what worked for me. Maybe they will work for you too?

In the beginning, I wasn't a writer. These words were originally just journaling that poured out of me. May these words pour into you. If you are ready to heal your disease of loneliness and achieve wholeness, then this book is for you. Perhaps, you can save yourself some pain by hearing about mine? I encourage you to ask yourself, what are you learning? Get an X-Ray of what's happening in you. I find that it is the best diagnostic tool— to look deep within. Ask yourself, what are you learning? What strategies are successful? (And write them down.) I'd love to hear from you — share with me at www.GraceWroldson.com

We help each other!
**Grace W. Wroldson**

# My Survival Strategies, My Pearls

*No grit. No pearl.*

Strategy:
✓ Find an Inner Substance

*"Pearls lie not on the seashore. If thou desirest one thou must dive for it."*
*— Chinese Proverb*

## Diving Deep Within

The pearl is one of nature's most prized secrets and its secret was all about survival.

**Do you see the pearl in you?**

Loving an alcoholic was a love that I lost myself in. I was like a piece of sand from the bottom of the sea that got trapped in an oyster. A part of me was upset that I had written my first book about loving an alcoholic. I never wanted to be known for that. I felt lost in the pages of that book because it still was about the alcoholic. I struggled to shift the focus to me. I was still trapped in the alcoholic dilemma.

After the breakup and after seven years of sobriety from codependency, I had moved on (with my Higher Power's help). I was living an empowered life and inspiring others. I wanted to be known for something better than a victim of a "love gone wrong." I didn't realize that I was being polished with a special coating. I had "pearls of wisdom" within me and I was being polished into a pearl myself.

# Was I the sand or the oyster?

My relationship with the alcoholic was painful and toxic. I did what any oyster would do with any irritant it can't expel (or gets stuck with), I coated it with my recovery efforts until it was contained. From there, a beautiful lesson to share and perhaps wear emerged. I found the same survival wisdom of a small mollusk from the depths of the ocean. I felt like I too was in a great big sea and deep in it. I was living on the bottom of the ocean floor. I was still in this alcoholic dilemma and had to raise a child. I had to learn to swim. Before I could swim, I needed to find a way to evolve and survive within the contaminated waters. I had to find some inner substance that would self-preserve and self-protect.

## Being Part of Nature

It sounds silly but I learned from the trials and tribulations of the oyster. I learned that we are all trying to survive and live in a big ocean. I am in a sea of many people with personalities that complement and contradict. Just like the oyster, I too, am part of nature. And in my lifetime I needed to learn to evolve and survive rough, toxic, and choppy waters. I learned that nature fills voids and I was one of the "void fillers" for the alcoholic. And yet, at the same time, he was filling a void in me that was carried over from my childhood. I wasn't filled with an inner substance, I had to create it.

## Do you Know How a Pearl is Formed?

The pearl is cocooned by a crystalline substance called nacre - a smooth lustrous coating. It is said to be lighter and stronger than concrete. I found my inner nacre and this was an inner substance that I could use to protect my interior. Little did I know, like the unsuspecting oyster, that when brought to the surface and light these would be beautiful precious gems of wisdom. It was wisdom that people would be drawn to. When alcoholism tried to invade, I applied another coating of my recovery (for protection). I was also coating my lessons with love, another powerful substance.

## Protection Against Invaders

I was drawn to the symbolic nature of how the pearl is created. There was beauty behind its defense mechanism. Something valuable is crafted miraculously out of trouble that enters the organism and because it is virtually helpless (can't swim away) and unable to expel the intruder, a magical pearl coating is applied. The coating is a special secret substance made of millions of microscopic crystals each aligned perfectly. When light passes along an axis of one, it's reflected and refracted to produce a tapestry of color. It takes several years to develop a pearl. And that's an important thing to keep in mind. It took me several years to learn my lessons and develop my strategies to survive.

If I was the oyster in the first part of my life, and if what was I doing was sitting on the ocean floor being a bottom-feeder, I wanted rise up, swim, change, and be a dolphin. I didn't want to be an oyster - I wanted to be free like a dolphin. I wanted to laugh, swim, experience joy and freedom. A new life appealed to me over remaining on the bottom of the ocean passively waiting for my next meal or invader. I knew that only a Power greater than myself and the readiness of my soul could change the kind of creature I am.

## With Recovery

With recovery, I applied coating after coating of my own special substance. My substances were made up of self-help, mentors, Twelve-Step meetings, spiritual studies, personal retreats, educational trainings, yoga, and new friends who believed in a Higher Power. I had to coat and protect myself against the effects of alcoholism on my and my child's life. I also applied layers of positive affirmations to keep myself firm. Then, I was able to make my own pearls of wisdom.

Grace W. Wroldson

## Polishing the Pearl

I learned from nature. I was fortifying my life by working my recovery program. I was becoming stronger. No alcoholic, no love. No alcoholism, no lessons. No problems, no pearl. No pain, no healing. No strategies, no survival. What's your pearl? Do you have a special substance for survival within you?

*"The rarest things in the world, next to a spirit of discernment, are diamonds and pearls."*
*— Jean de la Bruyere*

# A Smart Starter Strategy:
# ✓ Know the Problem(s)

✓ Understand Alcoholism,
✓ and Understand Yourself in Relation to It

✓ Understand Codependency,
✓ and Alcoholism as a Disease

*"Some people watch things happen,*
*Some people make things happen,*
*And some people wonder what happened?*
*I was one of the latter."*
*— AA speaker at an annual Al-Anon picnic*

## *It's the Approach That Matters*

## Why do I call alcoholism a family disease?

I choose to view and understand alcoholism as a disease. Why do I qualify alcoholism this way? Well, I discovered that there is an element of human compassion when I think in terms of alcoholism as an illness. For example, if someone had cancer, I wouldn't blame them, or be harsh. Cancer sufferers are suffering. Alcoholics in active alcoholism are suffering. There is no point in hurting the person more by blaming and shaming them for a sickness they didn't want. If a person is at the point of cancer or active alcoholism, I believe that no amount of blaming or coercing can undo what has been done. That mentality and approach adds more pain. So, I learned to view alcoholism as it was showing up (like a disease). Alcoholism was presenting itself to me as a chronic illness not someone's lack of willpower.

In order for me to treat the alcoholic with dignity, compassion, and respect, I chose to think of alcoholism as:

- A disease
- An illness
- A sickness
- A cancer
- A problem that someone is suffering from

What happens when I treated the alcoholic like he wanted to be sick?

Before realizing that the alcoholic didn't wake up every morning wanting to ruin our relationship, drink himself to death, and cause his own on happiness, I scolded, lectured, and often gave him the silent treatment. I blamed, shamed, and used all other kinds of hurtful tactics to try to get him to stop having this cancer. My behavior and anger towards alcoholism made our relationship worse. Looking back, I realize how unloving I was.

Besides all that unkind behavior, I also had to stop doing the following things:

- Stop trying to understand alcoholism perfectly
- Stop trying to figure out how to fix his alcoholism
- Stop trying to repair our relationship and skipping over the drinking problem
- Stop trying to be politically correct about this issue

**Refusing to Get Stuck**

I refused to get stuck on understanding something as complex as alcoholism. I decided (for myself) that no matter if alcoholism is or it isn't a disease the person under the influence of alcohol is toxic to themselves and to me. So, my approach is what mattered.

Also, for myself, I began to believe that alcoholism is not just a disease but also a spiritual crisis. It was similar to my toxic codependency as it was my own sickness and spiritual crisis. In an odd and paradoxical way our wounds matched. It was an alcoholic-codependent sickness that I came to call and know as the "family disease of alcoholism." I stopped blaming the alcoholic.

**Understand Codependency, and Alcoholism as a Disease**

**Where did I stunt my growth?**

To control the progression of alcoholism, I tried to learn all I could about it. It was an effort. But after spending the first ten years reading on the subject and attempting to understand alcoholism (which I discovered to be near impossible), I inadvertently stunted my own growth. I was stuck on trying to figure him out. I was stuck on what to call this disease. In hindsight, focusing on him was somehow safe in a sick way. So, truthfully, it was my codependency that stunted my growth. It stunted my growth to stay focused on him. I was acting like an emotional teenager in love— infatuated and obsessed. (While he was emotionally an irresponsible teenager enjoying drinking and refusing to get help.) My growth came when I was willing to face myself, look at myself, and look inside myself. I grew to love in new ways.

36

I also got stuck on having a Higher Power. I couldn't figure out what to call a power greater than myself to practice the Twelve Steps of Al-Anon. It stunted my growth to try to approach alcoholism in just a logical way.

## Love the person, hate the disease

*"Love recognizes no barriers. It jumps hurdles, leaps fences, penetrates walls to arrive at its destination full of hope."*
— *Maya Angelou*

After years loving him, followed by years hating him, I began to comprehend the saying, "love the person, hate the disease." I didn't love this cancer-like alcoholism. But I did love the alcoholic. That is before I lost respect for what the disease did to him. Then, when I was no longer in the relationship, I looked at myself and realized how angry I was with myself. I mistakenly projected that anger onto the alcoholic. I had not only led myself into a relationship like this but let myself down. I had to learn to love myself but hate this codependency sickness.

## But where did loving an alcoholic take me?

Loving an alcoholic took me to the root of my problems of codependency. I had a mental set-up. His alcoholism sent me the message that I had internal wounds. With the ability to shift my thinking I then could see the sick and suffering alcoholic was then a messenger of my wounds. I had to come to know the real nature of the problems I was facing in the alcoholic-codependent. Somewhere and sometime this all started. And I learned that our set up started before we joined together.

To avoid self-righteous separation of the alcoholic in my mind I had to start thinking in terms of:

- Us (and not "me-against-him")

- The alcoholic-codependent dynamic
- A family dilemma
- A family disease

By considering these aspects, I did the most loving thing I could do. I remained loving and compassionate towards the alcoholic while detaching and leaving the relationship. This was also how I was loving and compassionate towards myself as I suffered from codependency. The point is that I remained loving towards the both of us. What I know is that the approach I took mattered because of how I would treat us individually (and separately when we separated). I choose to treat this as a disease, illness, sickness, and family dilemma. Alcoholism was a disease that affected me. I came to know the problem(s). Then, I came to find the right solutions.

I stopped asking why the alcoholic was drinking and I came to ask myself the right question, "What does my disease demand?"

# The Codependent Spell

Are you under a spell?

*"I could not solve my problem of codependency*
*with the same codependent mind that created it."*
— Grace W. Wroldson

## *The Movie Star Spell*

I fell in love with him... then, I fell under the spell. It was so strong... so strong. I really needed to hold on to myself and know myself to stay straight, sane, and sober from it. But I didn't, I couldn't; I closed my eyes and inhaled all I could of him as he drank alcohol and fell under its control. He stood in the spotlight that I put on him. And so, I stood there "starstruck."

### What spell are you under?

I was under a "codependent spell." It was way beyond being blinded by love. This spell was a mixture of fantasy, lust, denial, longing, fear, self-will, and obsession. I was in a relationship with an alcoholic for fifteen years so my spell was heavy and dense. As my years under the spell added up, the more stages of my codependency I underwent, the more serious it became for me. I was deeply under it.

### Stages of Codependency

My codependency was activated with the chaos of "alcoholic-codependent" drama. I was fully active in my addiction to him as he was to alcohol. His alcoholic version of love helped me to stay under this spell, as well as, my codependent inability to let go. My listening to the alcoholic's sincere outpouring of emotion that I had thought was coming from his heart had me hooked. To me, he was like a movie star. I stopped everything to watch him perform. I often got high on his drama and gave him the whole stage. The love addict in me loved the addict in him. It was beyond entertainment for me - it was a full addiction.

## Not the Alcoholic's Fault

What I originally believed to be the alcoholic's fault (you know, for creating the dream that was just that a dream which he never followed through on), what I originally blamed him for (you know with his promises, appearances, and words which I craved to hear, by the way) — I woke up to realize were actually *my* issues. It surprised me to see that my own mind had cast the spell it ended up falling under. The conditions in my mind were ripe and right for the magic of alcoholic-love, leaving me spellbound. He had all the right words. I had all the right conditioning.

## What was I learning?

I was learning what a spell truly was. I learned that spells are real and not just something from a Harry Potter movie.

*Definition of a "spell":*
*"1 a : a spoken word or form of words held to have magic power*
*b : a state of enchantment*
*2 : a strong compelling influence or attraction"*
*— Merriam Webster online*

**Under the codependent spell I was…**

- Dating the same man over and over, expecting a different relationship
- Falling in love with his potential, even though it wasn't his true potential at all (just something I crafted and created for him in a fairytale that lived in my mind)
- Putting him on a pedestal while simultaneously putting myself down
- Being the same girl yet getting a new guy, and wanting a different experience while I was the same old me

## What is the codependent spell?

The codependent spell is like being charmed and wanting to be charmed so badly that we cast the spell ourselves with our own thoughts. In order to stay under this spell, I had to regularly practice several forms of denial. That was how I was able to live in a parallel reality for so long. I convinced myself that the drinking wasn't that bad, and we were headed to our castle. Definitely a fantasy.

I also learned that my codependency was a form of fear, not love. My codependent behaviors all stemmed from fear, too. So, my codependent spell was a strong spell of THE strongest stuff on the psyche: fear.

## My First Book of Lessons

In my first book, I looked at my life through the lens of learning my lessons to heal and overcome my codependency. All the lessons were part of my long-term healing process and building a new and better, long-term relationship with myself. Those original lessons were for living my life beyond the walls of my codependency. I was coming out of the spell and it was a struggle. I wrote my first book to start my sobriety from codependency.

I Love an Alcoholic, but Hated The Drinking

After years of recovery, I realized that it was crazy to minimize and disregard the things I was seeing the alcoholic do (like drinking and driving for example). For a time, during early recovery, waking up from the codependent spell and being able to see clearly it was both a blessing and a curse. I was seeing things about myself that I didn't like. But I also found out that once I was aware of this about myself, I could change. I needed to take responsibility for allowing someone to control me by waving a wand over me, so to speak. I took responsibility for showing up to the show, raising my hand, and volunteering myself to be hypnotized by a love spell. Sober living from codependency was a full-time job. I was learning to take responsibility for myself and the spellcasting habit of mine.

**In This Book of Strategies**

In this book, I share my survival strategies for stopping the casting of spells (and to stop going under this spell). I found a way to not fall under a codependent spell again and that's to stay awake, sane, and most importantly stay in recovery. If you are choosing to now live in reality, because the reality that you were creating under the codependent spell was becoming too painful then this may be a little book of recovery counterspells for you. I woke up to the fact that I too was responsible for our child being in a situation involving an alcoholic father. I was sick from my codependency. I had to face myself and be courageous about it.

**First Things First**

First, I needed to confess codependency and own my part in my problems. Otherwise I was blaming the alcoholic and focusing my happiness (and life) completely on him. In recovery, I had grown past the point of blaming when I grew my wings as shown in the first book. Read those 25+ powerful lessons in *So You Love an... Alcoholic? Lessons for a Codependent.* By healing and working recovery (and learning my lessons) I was refusing to allow my life to be all about the alcoholic.

Even more so, I was done saying no to others (which took a lot of energy) by setting up and maintaining good boundaries for myself (often with myself) so that I didn't have to say no that often. I was ready to start saying yes to myself and to my life. Are you ready to say "Yes!" to you?

## Taking Responsibility for Spell Casting

I had to take responsibility for my codependent spell. It was my issue. Not his. My mind created cognitive dissonance which was the codependency spell. I learned that cognitive dissonance is the ability of the mind to hold two conflicting, opposite thoughts at the same time. My mind was a master at manipulating me.

## Examples of my cognitive dissonance were:

"I love him." *and yet* "I hate him."
or
"I can't live without him." *and yet* "I can't live with him."

## Lulled Into Complacency

Even more so, over time, my love for him lulled me into complacency. I was on "human heroin" which was like a love drug. It was my drug of choice. To stay spelled (essentially drugged), I had to mold and fit data, filter date, and re-write data to get my fix. My addiction to him controlled me. And my addiction to control also controlled me. I was being controlled by codependency.

## Are you being controlled?

I learned that I was easily controllable being codependent. The alcoholic knew how I would react. The ways I was being controlled were clever. In my codependency, caring and controlling sometimes were the same thing to me.

Before recovery and before my awakening, I was:
- Controlled by my ingrained guilt.
- Controlled by my pride in my credibility and my integrity.
- Controlled by my fears of confrontation and abandonment.
- Controlled by my deep desires to get along and to be liked.
- Controlled by my love for him.
- Controlled by my sickness of self-doubt.
- Controlled, controlled, controlled!

You may want to stop right here and ask yourself: "Am I being controlled?"

**What broke the spell?**

When the fog lifts and when the cloud of denial evaporates from the codependent spell, there is an amazing clarity that is almost too vivid to withstand. What broke the spell for me? Hitting my bottom, a dark place where I sinned against my soul to try to save the relationship. Oh, and… the other woman. Yes, she helped break the spell, too. Today, I have learned to thank her and not to hate her. Another powerful spellbreaker was... having a baby. Having a child woke me up to realize that there was just too much at stake to play the alcoholic's drinking games anymore.

Losing myself to codependency was my greatest despair. Finding myself again, by practicing recovery was one of my greatest joys. Getting clear and away from my drug of choice (my relationship with him), cleared things up. The spell was broken.

*"Today I trust me. I trust in my perceptions. Today I will live my own truth that glows within, a life of no deceptions."*
*— Patricia Robin Woodruff*

**Can you see the spell you are under?**

I couldn't see the spell I was under. How could I? I also learned that I couldn't fix my codependent sickness with the same codependent mind that created it. I needed a recovery mind. I needed a new magician. A Higher Power and my soul became my source of love and counter magic for the codependent spell of fear. I learned to self-partner and partner with a Higher Power's powers.

*"No problem can be solved from the same level of consciousness that created it."*
—*Albert Einstein*

I encourage you to read my story, learn from my journey, find your recovery, and find your path to freedom. Here's how I overcame this codependent-alcoholic scenario and stayed sober. You can too!

*"The greatest thing a human soul ever does in this world is to see something and tell what it saw in a plain way."*
— *John Ruskin*

# Someone's Soul

We were intertwined together by the invisible threads of our souls
for we shared a sacred tapestry called Life.

*What was happening with our souls?*

Standing there soul to soul,
someone's soul grew,
someone's soul stopped,
then someone's soul had had enough.

This was as far as our souls would stay stitched,
when I saw the sickness in our souls surface.

After the unraveling, my soul sat... and sat... and sat.
My soul sat curled up on the couch alone.
My soul stared out windows seeing nothing.
Our time was up,
my soul had suffered enough.

My soul had been shaped
but something had shifted and snapped.
From suffering too severe,
my soul forced a shut down
to sleep.

Now, my soul sought separation.
What my soul needed now was to savor the sun of its own sunshine,
not the shadows of another's sickness.

Uncovering myself, I saw that my soul carried the stain of my choices.
I wove in some solitude as a cradle.
I followed a different thread to craft sacred soul-time.
In a prayer to myself, I declared my soul contract complete.

Someone's soul had been spared.
— *Grace W. Wroldson*

# Strategy #1:
# Courageously Confess Codependency, Survive Yourself

✓ Know Yourself and
✓ Survive Being You

**Codependent Confessions**

*"Once they have been affected—once "it" sets in—codependency takes on a life of its own. It is similar to catching pneumonia or picking up a destructive habit. Once you've got it, you've got it. If you want to get rid of it, YOU have to do something to make it go away. It doesn't matter whose fault it is. Your codependency becomes your problem; solving your problems is your responsibility."*

*— Melody Beattie, Codependent No More:*
*How to Stop Controlling Others and Start Caring for Yourself*

## *Cleansing My Psyche*

I finally stopped asking if I could survive the alcoholic's alcoholism and asked myself, "Can I survive my own codependency issues?"

When I was trying to survive the alcoholic relationship and when I was focusing on him, I never looked at myself. Not even a glance. I was caught up in my own codependent craziness circling around him. The last six months of our relationship, I was in a full-blown codependent crisis. Our relationship was failing and I could feel it. I finally identified my own problems within myself.

I was suffering from severe internal, toxic energy which was destroying me. The chemicals associated with resentment, loss, victimization, and martyrdom were coursing through my system and breaking me down. My codependency created a blind spot, and so I could not see the real issues from my disoriented, weakened state. I could not see the things that were so obvious to others because I was codependent and confused. **The fact was, I couldn't get any solutions for myself by focusing on him.** I was trying to survive alcoholism but not realizing that I had to survive myself. I was codependently toxic even to myself. If I was going to label him an alcoholic and call this an alcoholism problem to get the right help, then it occurred to me that I had to name myself, too. I had codependency—completely.

*"...codependency - the concept of losing oneself in the name of helping another - "*
— *Melody Beattie, Codependent No More*

Step One of the Twelve Steps is about admitting when life becomes unmanageable. My life was unmanageable with my codependency issues. I had to confess that I was always putting him before me. I had to confess that I was unmanageable even to myself. I couldn't handle my anxiety. I myself was unmanageable emotionally, never mind my life. It wasn't easy loving an alcoholic for as long as I did. It wasn't easy being codependently me for as long as I was - that's for sure. I was paying the consequences for the alcoholic and I had to stop. I was paying the consequences of being myself. But how could I stop being myself?

**A Compassion Cleanse**

Pre-recovery, I secretly and subconsciously went on anti-alcoholism campaigns with my codependency. What was that? It involved dumping alcohol down the drain, never taking a drink, staying away from bars, declining invites to drinking parties, and being tough on the subject of alcohol use with everyone. I was unaware that I was even up to this madness. Also, I was passive-aggressive, trying to get my needs met by the alcoholic. I had codependent confessions that I needed to make. I made a formal admission that I was guilty of codependency.

*"Tell me, is there someone in your life who's been sharing your life too closely? A friend or a loved one? Is there someone who's been taking up your time and not giving any of it back?"*
— *Alexandra Kleeman, You Too Can Have a Body Like Mine*

When I found out just how conniving my codependency was, and after I confessed my codependency to a safe person in the program, I had to apply some compassion to myself because back then I was in a completely clueless state and could not recognize how I was harming myself with my codependent behaviors (ie; caretaking, justifying, and denial). I was sharing my life too closely with an alcoholic who wasn't giving anything back. Initially, when I woke up to my role as a conniving codependent, I was disappointed in myself. I was also very hard on myself for this behavior. Where was the compassion for myself? I was suffering so much from my codependency that often left me lonely, heartbroken, and destroyed. But, compassion became a cleanse. When I applied compassion, I felt cleansed of the poisonous internal, toxic emotional states. I found some sympathy for my own suffering.

*"If you ever feel the person in your life needs rescuing, particularly from him or herself - beware. Codependency is rearing its head again."*
— *David Stafford, Codependency: How to Break Free and Live Your Own Life*

## Toxically Unaware

Before recovery, I was beyond naive. I was toxically unaware with my many blind spots that were putting me under a codependent spell. As my spell broke, I began to see that my problem was not so much out "there" (it appeared to be - the alcoholic) as it was in "here" (in me). With a heightened consciousness came more awareness of my codependency. Confessing codependency is when I stopped my struggle using self-righteousness. Confessing humbled me as I was realizing that I was only human, just like the alcoholic.

I had other confessions to make, but confessing my codependency was confessing that I had problems that were much like a disease. My disease took me down to doing things outside of my integrity. For example, there was a part of me that knew not to have a child with an active alcoholic. Deep down, I felt it was wrong to bring a child into this mess. So why did I still do it? I learned that I had a codependent sickness and that I needed help. Even though I was not religious, I was confessing this "sin" against myself because I felt that I had sinned against my own soul.

### My Lesson:

✓ Confess my codependency, survive myself
✓ (Survive being me by knowing myself)

I sought the Twelve-Step rooms of recovery in Al-Anon. First, for his issue with drinking and then with my issue of being adversely affected. I became anxiously controlling because the disease felt so out of control. By practicing my unhealthy codependency, I was suffering assaults to my soul as I betrayed myself daily in that relationship. Confessing was like a cleanse of my psyche. I learned that telling someone what I had done in a state of codependency cleaned off some of my sins against myself. Confession cleansed my soul.

### A Codependent Cinder Girl

I thought that surviving an alcoholic relationship was an extreme challenge. **What didn't occur to me, until I could see my codependency tendency clearly, was that I had to survive myself and my issues.** My issues led me to... caretaking of others, controlling others, and constantly involving myself with others (to my detriment). I needed to survive the financial problems that I accumulated as the result of being so overly giving out of a sense of guilt and complete lack of self-preservation. I needed to survive my complex intertwining with others in my life (an attachment disorder) that took up so much time that I couldn't clean my own house because I was caring and cleaning for others, like a Cinderella.

*"No one is coming to save you. No one has a magic wand they can wave to make everything the way you hope. No one can save you from yourself. Stop being your own worst enemy. Work with yourself and not against. Love yourself. Be honest about what and who you are. Only you can save yourself from yourself by learning to cooperate with yourself. By learning to see yourself with grace, compassion, and love. By being your own friend."*

*— Akiroq Brost*

## Recovery From Codependency, Cleaning Up My Susceptibilities

When I realized how bad my codependency was and nobody was going to appear and save me (especially not the alcoholic), I centered my life on recovering from the effects of alcoholism. I was on my knees scrubbing my dirty floors from being affected by alcoholism and very subservient to the alcoholic-codependent dysfunction. However, my recovery morphed into recovering from my own codependency because when the alcoholic was not around, I still had problems. I had to turn the focus onto myself and see what my original vulnerabilities were and resolve them. I had to stop focusing on helping others so that I could focus on figuring myself out (or at least starting identifying/uncovering who I was). With my recovery from codependency, I was learning to be authentic and unaffected by others. I was learning about my own "dirt." I was cleaning myself up in recovery.

*"He who knows others is wise; he who knows himself is enlightened."*

*— Lao Tzu*

## Flushing Then Plunging Back Up My Potential

Before the alcoholic- codependent relationship, I had so much potential. One Halloween, for trick or treat, my mom and I were proudly walking my daughter around the neighborhood that I happily grew up in. We came to a neighbor who was a successful, well-known attorney. He had raised three daughters who were away in college when I was a young girl. He was a happily married man and had a beautiful house and a huge garden in his backyard. Lucky for me, he loved children. Often, I spent the boring parts of my summer in his backyard, following him around like the fourth daughter he never had and learning all kinds of things. I had so many fond memories.

But showing up at his door as a struggling single mom with an alcoholic's child and living in low-income housing in town embarrassed me. My mother introduced my daughter and talked about how smart she is and how well she is doing in school and is about to enter kindergarten. He said he was not surprised. He looked down and began to tell my daughter that I was one of the smartest little girls he had known. He proceeded to tell a story of how I fixed something mechanical of his that was broken when I was six years old. He went on to say how he watched me (by reading the local papers) earn top honors in high school and at the local college. Having flashbacks of all he recalled, I stayed at the end of his driveway hiding under my hat and said nothing. I walked away with tears streaming down my face. I was glad it was dark out because I could cry unnoticed. I felt like I had flushed all my potential down the toilet. I had to get my plunger and use it to plunge myself back up. After all those draining years in an alcoholic relationship, was my potential still there?

## Cleaning by Forgiving Myself

Could I forgive my codependency? I often wondered how recovering alcoholics could forgive their alcoholism and what it led them to do (and not do). For me to be able to return to the alcoholic codependent relationship, I was always forgiving him. **So, if I had forgiven him hundreds of times for what he and his alcoholism did, then I knew I could forgive myself for the hundreds of mistakes I had made.** When I started to realize my part in the alcoholic-codependent problem, I was initially very hard on myself. I had to confess my codependency to myself and a few trusted friends also suffering from this condition. Their compassion for my struggle helped me develop compassion for myself. Through this compassion, I was able to reach forgiveness. Most importantly, I saw that I needed to survive being me.

*"Know thyself and all will be revealed."*
— *Pamela Theresa Loertscher*

I had to take my mop and stop cleaning up the alcoholic's mess and, instead, clean up after myself and mop my own floor. I had way too many triggers and traumas that would come up and put me in a reactive state, disrupting my ability to respond from a mature, solid sense of self. When I betrayed myself, it chipped away at my soul. When I realized that I had soul parts missing from being in an alcoholic relationship, I sought out ways to call them back. After the alcoholic relationship, I never wanted to give myself away like that again. As I healed and grew stronger, I wanted to keep parts of me —just for myself.

After having such a bad existence with the alcoholic, I was determined to live and have a good life. But first I needed to do years of healing. I sought out many different healing modalities some very new-age, some ancient. To get myself back, I went so far as to seek therapy through shamanic energy healing sessions called soul retrievals. I took myself to several sessions with a shaman who has survived an alcoholic relationship herself. When I learned how to do soul retrievals on myself, I could call back the part of me that was given over to the alcoholic and create a safe and secure home within myself. When I got healthier, I no longer gave parts of me away. I stayed solid in my sense of self and said, "No" often. What was interesting was that from a self-empowered state, having good functioning boundaries with others, for the most part, I only had to say "No" to myself. I had evolved past blaming the alcoholic and was owning my codependent conditioning. I was being codependent and I realized that I needed to survive my codependency. I became ready to be a safe place for myself and practice self-preservation.

I asked myself, "If I had the capacity in my heart to love a man so much that I went to the depths of his hell to try to help him... think of how much I could love and help myself?"

Without a relationship, I had inner codependent urges that were screaming at me to find relief in another man. It was a codependent craving, coaxing me into a relationship where I would get lost by giving and giving again. Things that were so utterly confusing in the relationship only became clear to me when I was out of the relationship. I realized that when I was answering the alcoholic's screams, I stopped listening to my own and became focused on hearing his. It was a twisted cowardly way to work around my pain and not have to face it. Focusing on his needs and not having to look at myself was pseudo relief for me but definitely not a healthy kind of relief. I also noticed that the effects of the disease of alcoholism multiplied the intensity of my own shortcomings. When his problems grew larger, so did mine. I was too attached. However, after learning about myself by working the program, I could understand that my problems began long before alcoholism came into my life. The screaming didn't stop until I reached recovery.

## My Life Was A Mess

In the relationship, and for years after the relationship, my inner-life was a mess; so it followed that, consequently, my outer-life was also a mess. My internal clutter consisted of serious self-doubt, lack of self-love, not believing in myself, etc. I had spent years training myself to clean up after him and his mess, so I knew I could apply that same care to myself. Turns out that alcoholism was just a mirror reflecting back my ever-present, already-existing codependency. When I learned to look into the reflection at myself, I could see the mental clutter of my past in the background - behind me. I needed help. I needed to clean-up, get saved, and become whole.

*"Being kind, gentle, empathetic and helpful should not be at the cost of your own growth. Most certainly help others, lend a shoulder to the wheel when necessary but don't ignore yourself in the bargain. Strike a balance, help others and help yourself too."*

*— Latika Teotia*

Once I admitted that I too needed saving, I could focus on myself and do for me what I had done for him. I could take care of myself, keep myself whole, and give myself the things I needed— things that I had wanted and never received from the alcoholic. When I confessed my codependency, it allowed me to focus on the real issues that plagued me and caused so much of my hurt. I no longer lived with an active alcoholic. Actually, I lived alone. So who was hurting me now?

## Erased Myself

What my codependency essentially did was erase me. By giving all my attention to the alcoholic and being hell bent on saving the relationship, I erased who I was. I gave and gave, focused and focused (on him), and lost the person I was. And I also lost the person I was meant to be. These were painful realizations. I couldn't be me and live in my truth with the lies that alcoholism told. I had to find some small part of myself that hadn't left or been given away. I had to find a part that stayed and saw all my soul-loss and suffering. There, I found what was left of my soul. I had to hang onto my soul with a Higher Power and let go of the alcoholic that I loved.

## Detoxing From The Alcoholic And Undergoing Withdrawal

To stop hurting myself with him, I needed to do a detox from the alcoholic. I went "no contact" and then went through terrible withdrawal. But being honest with myself, digging down deep within myself, I discovered that his alcoholism was not the root of my problem. The root of my problems were my traumas trapped inside of me. They were in charge of me making my decisions based in fear. I discovered that it was not the truth about someone else that would make me free. It was the truth about myself that would make me free and that would set me free. I had an addiction to loving him and codependency issues consuming me. That was my truth.

My new and next question became... How do I survive myself while living with me full-time? I had first asked a Higher Power to shield me from the disease of alcoholism, but how do I seek cover from myself (from codependency and my inner love addict)? I was with me all of the time! The answer finally came when I asked that question. I was to go into the depths of my own personal hell (within myself), heal my traumas and wounds, and then I heard something inside myself say... "Change!" Healing, changing, and looking at my traumas was intense. So, I got a sponsor in the program to work through the Steps. In deep confession, I had to learn to ask my soul and a Higher Power to help me.

So, I said to myself, "Be courageous!"

*"The only way that we can live, is if we grow. The only way that we can grow is if we change. The only way that we can change is if we learn. The only way we can learn is if we are exposed. And the only way that we can become exposed is if we throw ourselves out into the open. Do it. Throw yourself."*
— C. JoyBell C.

## My Take-a-away Strategy: Courageously Confess Codependency

I courageously confessed my codependency and began to survive myself - with all my codependent tendencies (and where those led me in my life). I had to know myself better and survive being me in my world. I made codependent confessions to clean my psyche. I focused on the problems I was having, instead of the problems the alcoholic was having. I healed my life.

❖ If you would like to read some of my other survival strategies and read FREE excerpts of my other books, please visit my website at: www.GraceWroldson.com

# Strategy #2:
# Fearlessly Focus on the "You" Factor

✓ Redefine the "You" Variable
✓ Improve Yourself

*"I learned again and again in my life, until you get your own act together, you're not ready for Big Love. What you're ready for is one of those codependent relationships where you desperately need a partner."*

— Bruce H. Lipton, The Honeymoon Effect: The Science of Creating Heaven on Earth

## Living an Equation for a Successful Life

**I asked myself, "Why didn't my life add up?"**

I was good at math but for some reason things were not adding up well with the alcoholic. My codependent life with the alcoholic relationship didn't add up to love, happiness, contentment, and inner peace. When I figured in the alcoholic, I was living an equation in my life that was just not equaling what I wanted. So, I added in his possible recovery in AA and couples counseling, but no matter how hard I tried to set my life up for success with him; something was always inherently wrong with my equation. Back then, it was like sitting in school trying to solve a really complex math problem. I stayed late, erased, made revisions, and desperately added and subtracted, trying to get my life to work with the alcoholic. I never realized that the common denominator was "Me," and that something very significant was missing.

I Love an Alcoholic, but Hated The Drinking

**My early life-equations looked something like this:**

**Me + The Alcoholic ≠ Love, Happiness, Contentment, and Inner Peace**

Another attempt after the breakup with alcoholic looked like this:

**Me + Healthy Eating + More Exercise + More Friends − (The Alcoholic)**

**≠ Love, Happiness, Contentment, and Inner Peace (either!)**

Something was missing from my equation of living. I discovered that one thing I was missing was a Higher Power. This is what I eventually came to call "God" (my Higher Power).

**Finding The Right Constants**

I had spiritual friends who strongly believed in a Higher Power. They seemed less scared of life and more sure of themselves. I thought it would be nice to allow myself to lean on some type of "sustaining infinite" rather than a fallible man or my own "fair-weather" willpower. My willpower had a tendency to come and go depending on the moment, my emotional state, and other variables. I would be plus or minus one minute and then multiplication the next. **This is why I had to find the right constant - something unchangeable.** That something was a Higher Power. I learned to add my Higher Power's will for me and simply strive to follow HP's instruction toward better living. My Higher Power had to remain a constant, in addition to my recovery.

**Was my whole search about finding the right equation for life?**

By manually trying to add up my life, I set myself up for the danger of expecting a man to replace the sick one I had (to equal my happiness). I also learned that this was not a good equation for life either:

**Me + A Different/"Better" Man**
**≠ Love, Happiness, Contentment, and Inner Peace**

I was unrealistic with my expectations of life. I wanted simple, solvable solutions to my complex life-math. Dating other men after ending the relationship with the alcoholic showed me that no man would be a perfect addition. Thus my effort to replace one man for another was just bad thinking on my part. I was a stubborn student.

A better replacement for a man in my life was a relationship with my Higher Power. This new, powerful relationship led me to a loving relationship with myself. Even more so, the "Me" part of the equation had to be broken out "to see the work behind it". This made sense because I knew that I could not heal my codependent "diseased mind" with my same diseased mind. I needed mental interventions to my mental-math. I needed a Divine intervention.

*"I could not solve my codependent mind with the same mind that created my codependency."*
*— Grace W. Wroldson*

## Finding Out That I Was A Variable

In an equation, a constant is the value that is NOT changeable. I found my Higher Power to be that constant. A Higher Power was untouched by the disease of alcoholism, as opposed to "Me," I had been touched. I recognized myself (the "Me") as variable because I could change. **I had complete control in determining my value and how I impacted my equation.** In addition, I was able to change the "Me" variable to get different results in my life by adding another important constant — My Recovery.

## Finding Out That I Was The Common Denominator

*"You are the only common denominator in everything that has happened to you in life,*
*be it good or bad. To learn/grow from these experiences, you must accept the role you played in each of them."*
*— A.C. Anderson*

59

The truth was, I was adding sick codependency to everything when I added myself into my life. I needed time to myself, away from being caught up in the hype and fairy-tales of ultimate relationship success. I had to put down the quick-fix how-to-get-the-love-I-want books. My inner love-addict was hooked on quick success guides that claimed true love was as easy as 1, 2, 3. In my old life, I was looking for love through multiple choice answers. I learned that the "Me" factor was just as important as subtracting a toxic alcoholic relationship from my life. I was multiplying myself and my sickness out into every relationship. So, I couldn't find the love I wanted.

**My Lesson:**

✓ Focus on the "Me" factor
✓ Redefine "Myself" as a variable

Even with life-math, I could not rely solely on my mind to figure its way out of something it figured its way into (an alcoholic relationship). When I tried to reason with something that was unreasonable (my codependent thinking), I kept getting stuck on the problem. My codependency had an unreasonable quality, especially when it was determined to be happy after leaving the alcoholic. I also could not solve the problem by focusing on the problem. I had to switch and focus on the solutions. One solution was a Higher Power because that was not the variable "Me." So, what was my Higher Power? Well, I knew what it was not: it was not the alcoholic. So, I stopped adding him into my life equations.

*"Life is a math equation. In order to gain the most, you have to know how to convert negatives into positives."*
*— Anonymous*

## My Math

To heal and change, I had to take a deeper look at what comprised of "Me." I had to focus on myself. I was the variable in my algebra. I had to work on myself. I had to unravel and explore the parts that totaled "Me." In school, I learned that, when it came to math equations, one side had to equal the other to be balanced. Well, I wanted love, contentment, happiness, and inner peace on the other side of the equal sign; so I had to get my side of this equation cleaned up of all the pencil marks and mistakes. I realized that I had to first have what I wanted (totaled within me) on *this* side of the equation. Understanding what defined "Me" was as important as subtracting a toxic alcoholic relationship from my life.

*"I was exhilarated by the new realization that I could change the character of my life by changing my beliefs. I was instantly energized because I realized that there was a science-based path that would take me from my job as a perennial "victim" to my new position as 'co-creator' of my destiny."*
*— Bruce Lipton (Prologue, xv)*

I needed to start again "from scratch" with "Me" to get the results I wanted. I asked myself, "What made up "Me?" I further asked, "What if I added my recovery?" I needed to ask and answer, "How can I improve myself, right now?"

## My final functional equations became:

$$Me^{HIGHER POWER} + My\ Recovery = Me\ (redefined)$$
$$The\ New\ Me + Any\ Situation/Relationship = Love,\ Happiness,$$
$$Contentment\ and\ Inner\ Peace$$

*"Changing yourself changes everything."*
*— Bryant McGill, Existence*

So, I said to myself, "Be fearless!"

**My Take-a-away Strategy: Fearlessly Focus on the "Me" Factor**

I fearlessly focused on the "Me" factor and redefined the "Me" variable to change the circumstances of my life. I improved myself and then I began living an equation for a successful life. My life began to work in the ways I wanted it to.

❖ If you would like to read some of my other survival strategies and read FREE excerpts of my other books, please visit my website at: www.GraceWroldson.com

# Insight

*Into Myself I See*

If insight is true sight that looks within, here is what I saw...

My ego wants to have
My soul wants to share and serve
My spirit wants to inspire
My mind wants to know
My heart wants to love
My Life wants to serve a purpose
My psyche wants meaning
My soul wants symbols
My mind wants the truth
My being wants to be
My codependency wants to be free
My child wants to be loved
My love addict wants another high
My hatred wants to be humbled
My truth wants to be validated
My suffering wants to be for a greater purpose
My voice wants to speak and save the children.

If insight is sight that looks in, that's what I saw.
It was that simple.

— *Grace W. Wroldson*

# Strategy #3:
# Tenaciously Learn from Life

**The Lessons are More Important Than You Might Think**
   ✓ Detach or Die
   ✓ Extract the Learning

*"Nothing ever goes away until it has taught us what we need to know."*
— *Pema Chödrön, When Things Fall Apart: Heart Advice for Difficult Times*

**I asked myself, "Am I learning, like *really* learning my lessons?"**

## *Getting to the Heart of the Matter*

I needed to learn. I needed to learn my lessons because my life depended on it. Watching the disease of alcoholism overtake the alcoholic broke my heart. Watching how my own codependency led me to betray my own soul broke my heart even more. Being pregnant, alone, and scared with an active alcoholic's child woke me up to the realization that perpetuating my problems didn't just stop at my broken-heart; now someone else's little heart could be broken from being in this toxic relationship. Someone else would now have to pay the price of my inability to let go of an unhealthy relationship. As I began to look more closely at myself, I realized my life was complicated by my own doing. This was because (pre-recovery) I wasn't learning the important lessons in my life, so my situation became… life or death. I had to detach, or not only was I going to die but the little life inside me would die too. There were two of us hanging onto all of my life choices. Someone else's life depended on my "heart choice." Working hard to try to improve the alcoholic relationship (all by myself) meant I wasn't learning. I needed to figure out what my lessons were and finally learn them!

*"Though nobody can go back and make a new beginning... Anyone can start over and make a new ending."*
— *Chico Xavier*

## Cutting The Heart-Strings, Learning Detachment

I learned that it was dangerous for me to be around him. My heart was beating and breaking for all the wrong reasons. My heart loved him so much, and so my mind couldn't logically argue an emotion it couldn't understand. I felt deep love so strongly for the sick and suffering alcoholic that it often took over my mind. That's why I had to cut off the heart of my own addiction to the alcoholic or end up possibly having a miscarriage. Thankfully at this point, we had already broken up for the last and final time - just three months prior to me discovering that I was surprisingly, unexpectedly expecting. Sometimes timing is everything.

I only had to deal with two interactions with my alcoholic ex at the doctor's office, nauseated from the first trimester, before I went completely "no contact" with him. I was respectful enough to contact him and let him know that I was pregnant and respectful enough to let him know that the pregnancy wasn't going as medically smooth as one would hope due to some unexplained bleeding. I really wanted him to care and was looking for a caring response from him. I was anxiously wondering... would my baby make it? But the alcoholic was anxiously wondering if I would take him back because of this. Because, well... I usually always did.

Three days after my positive pregnancy test happened to be Mother's Day - a special day; a day that I had always dreamed of. I wanted to be a mother. But it was on Mother's Day, 2011, when I had an episode of what we all assumed was a full miscarriage. The on-call weekend obstetrician advised that there was nothing that could be done for me and the baby. I was terrorized by the thought that it was my first time being a mother and on my first Mother's Day, I was losing that

66

privilege. The on-call doctor advised me to come in for an appointment on Monday and check for a heartbeat. I don't know why, but I invited the alcoholic.

*"The wound is where the light enters you."*
*— Rumi*

## A Low Heart Beat

When, to everyone's surprise, there was a low heartbeat still remaining after the bleeding episode, we were advised to come in for an appointment every two weeks. I was told that first trimester miscarriages are completely normal, and it's the body's way of releasing if things weren't going well or set up right (the doctor had no idea of our drama and assumed we were walking in together as a couple). The doctor's words were meant to offer me assurance that my body had a maternal intelligence and all would be well and for the best. But where was my maternal intelligence regarding the alcoholic's ability to be a healthy parent? This became an expensive lesson in letting go because my inability to let go of the alcoholic was going to impact someone else - my baby.

While pregnant, I quickly learned that even a tiny amount of stress was too much to add to morning sickness and a complicated pregnancy. So, if the alcoholic spoke one negative word, my system screamed (and I strangely started to physically bleed). So, I had to distance myself. The complicated pregnancy kept me away from my alcoholic ex. That was a hidden gift that I often look back on in wonder and astonishment. Once the bleeding stopped, once I realized that I was given the gift of a precious child to love and the pregnancy was going full-term, I did not want to lose the baby, and so I loved it enough to leave that relationship behind - for good - and not go back. It was a "do or die" situation; it was definitely detach or die, literally, for both of us. What I didn't realize was that I would soon be correcting my choice of words because it was going to be "our baby," for I had to share a child with an active alcoholic.

## A Magical, Maternal Moment

On a lonely drive back from the third doctor's appointment (by myself), with a heartbeat still hanging on, despite all the unexplained hemorrhaging; I asked the child-to-be in my womb a question (as if it could hear me). I asked the very deep questions of, "Why have you come now? Why now, when we are done with the relationship and through with each other?" A part of me was still wondering about the timing and playing with the idea of what it would be like if the pregnancy happened while we had still been together. Could that have been my happily-ever-after with the alcoholic? Would having a child together make the alcoholic wake-up and stop drinking?

I wasn't expecting an answer, nor was I expecting any sort of feeling from within. But I will never forget a small, sure, and gentle voice that I felt come from the intelligence of a tiny life-form with the slow heart-beat. I felt my womb answer back, "I couldn't come any sooner. I wouldn't have made it if you were attached to Dad." I was amazed. Was that the baby, or my inner voice? I quickly decided it didn't matter. It was the absolute truth. Children, no matter how old, be it first trimester or six years old, have intelligence. By asking this question, I felt like I had finally tapped into that intelligence that runs the universe and creates life. I finally learned the lesson and the true value of detachment.

*"And once the storm is over, you won't remember how you made it through, how you managed to survive. You won't even be sure, whether the storm is really over. But one thing is certain. When you come out of the storm, you won't be the same person who walked in. That's what this storm's all about."*

*— Haruki Murakami*

**Cutting The Cords**

A curious thing happened when I unplugged from the alcoholic. All the life lessons that I was refusing to learn (so that I could stay with him, or take him back) came rushing out. Labeling my lessons is what erupted out of me when I separated from the relationship. As I wrote, I saw pieces of my wisdom circulating onto the pages I journaled. Cutting myself off from the alcoholic and my addiction to him (which was acted out in my acute codependency) gave me clarity. When I severed my heart strings connected to him, my heart stopped beating solely for him; my heart started beating for my baby. I wrote my lessons down so I could get to the heart of the matter (with me). Learning my lessons was how I made lemonade out of the lemons of my life. Learning my lessons birthed a new me.

*"Instead of worrying about what you cannot control, shift your energy to what you can create."*
— *Roy T. Bennett, The Light in the Heart*

I discovered that the lesson was important, but not so much the details of how I learned it. Many of my readers from my first book wanted personal anecdotes to hear how I comprehended and internalized these lessons, but they were personal, and I wasn't sure if it was necessary to share. I realized that I wasn't just loving an alcoholic and trying to leave him, I was learning my life lessons. The point was to learn the lessons however I could and with whatever was in front of me. I learned that light entered my heart when I lovingly let the alcoholic go - for the sake of all of us. I also learned to love myself and our child from a new heart-space and with the light and love of a Higher Power.

**Examining My Heart**

In my recovery, I dug deeper into myself and not the alcoholic. I stopped trying to make sense of how he functioned as well as his extreme dysfunction. I was determined to look inward (at myself) and made myself matter most. I began looking at the exact nature of my wrongs and not the details. I looked at why I was in a hurry trying to have a baby with the alcoholic the last six months of our relationship. I looked at what my heart was claiming to love about him. I looked at my definition of love and saw that I had confused love with pity. I came to look at my situation of loving an alcoholic archetypally instead of personally. There were so many life-lessons available for learning within the alcoholic-codependent functional dysfunction.

As things became clear, I allowed the alcoholic to be a reference point, or more like a reflection-point, of what was happening inside of me. The alcoholic was a mirror for me. I came to see that my childhood, traumas, past, and patterns comprised my codependency. These trapped energies were what needed to be "up-leveled" and brought into my awareness so that I could heal and then transform them into wisdom that could serve my life.

*"You are here, alive and awake and for whatever reasons you have fought your battles, it's time to start focusing on what strengths pulled you up when the entire world had knocked you down. That's where the virtue in self grows."*
— *Nikki Rowe*

## Extract The Lesson

My lesson objective became to name the lesson as I learned it. After I went through some learning-time in the alcoholic relationship, or alone (as a codependent in craving-mode), I labeled it. I named the lesson that was just taught to me by Life School. These lessons were what I wanted to *finally* learn. I'd stop at the end of sections of my life including surgery, court, and other life-trouble and then asked myself, "Now, what was it that I just learned?" It was the best question to end with, no matter how things turned out.

### My Lesson:
✓ Learn My Lessons!

**If I had a thesis for a doctorate, it would have been not the examination of the workings of the alcoholic, nor how to love an active alcoholic successfully - the right way - nor how to have a successful codependent relationship and be happy with an alcoholic, but rather it would have detailed what the complex inner workings of me were.** I had come to know myself deeply in my own heart. I had finally stopped blaming the alcoholic for why I didn't have a healthy, happy love life. I FINALLY learned to ask myself, "What was my part in this mess?" I learned to ask myself, "Did I learn my lesson?"

*"If I had the ability to love a man this much, imagine how much I could love myself?"*
*— Grace W. Wroldson*

So, I said to myself, "Be tenacious!"

**My Take-a-away: Tenaciously Learn From Life**

I became tenacious. I tenaciously learned from life. I realized that the lessons that I was learning were crucial for me to make it to a better life. I made the lessons important and I extracted the learning from them. I began to detach so I wouldn't die. I got into the heart of the matter with myself.

❖ If you would like to read some of my other survival strategies and read FREE excerpts of my other books, please visit my website at: www.GraceWroldson.com

# Strategy #4:
# Unstoppably Continue with Your Recovery

✓ Keep Working the Steps
✓ Stay in Program,
✓ Practice Step Twelve
✓ You Are Needed,
✓ Pay it Forward

**I asked myself, "Can it be all over now that I am not in a relationship with an alcoholic?"**

## *Being Needed*

I wasn't in an alcoholic relationship anymore. I was free from him and had my own life to live. Alcoholism was not in my home nor in my face. I didn't even have any alcohol in my kitchen cabinets for cooking. And I liked it that way! I lived as a single mom and there wasn't a man in my house to answer to or have to take care of with traditional wifely duties. I felt relief because I had relieved myself of those obligations and chores by leaving the alcoholic. So, I wondered if the chaos, drama, and confusion would now be over. Could I stop attending Al-Anon, resume my life, and stop going to therapy. Was the war finally over?

### Don't Stop Working The Program

What I didn't know was that when I stopped working the program, I slipped back into the same internal setup that was my codependency. Slipping back into the old version of me set me up for another alcoholic relationship! Surprisingly, unfortunately, and sadly, sometimes my next relationship was with the same alcoholic. I needed to stay in program and keep practicing my recovery for myself to stay sober from my own love addiction. I couldn't have long-term success if I just took what the program had to offer for my alcoholic situation, but didn't stay to help the newcomer. Looking back, I now see how selfish that was of me.

## Practice Step Twelve

Giving, which is part of Step Twelve of the Twelve Steps, was a way to always remember where I came from. Yes, I had survived a relationship with an alcoholic. Yes, I had survived the bad breakup, terrible loneliness, financial devastation, and the constant consequences of his family completely divorcing and shunning me even though we were never married. Yes, I was surviving rounds of court battles with my attorney to keep our child safe and out of an alcoholic home. Yes, I survived what my codependency had me do, which was very close to giving my life away. Yes, but I was still me. I still had codependency issues. However, I had a firm resolve to not self-harm again and I still had my recovery because I stayed in the program. I needed to stick with the things that worked and keep working it. Originally, I was going to Al-Anon thinking I was saving the alcoholic and he was worth it. But I stayed for myself because I finally decided I was worth it.

## Paying It Forward

My sponsor said, "one of the reasons that I stayed in recovery was because I couldn't pay it back, I had to pay it forward." My sponsor also explained, "The people who helped me when I came in were no longer in program because they moved away or had passed away, so I couldn't give it back - I had to pay it forward." I knew that I was fortunate to have such a dedicated sponsor to help me through my most recent decade of the program. As much as I thought I was lucky, I knew that I hand selected that sponsor because of the strength and wisdom I heard shared at the meetings. I was inspired by my sponsor's consistency, dedication, and willingness to listen to and help other sick and suffering Al-Anoners and witness (without judgement) all the Al-Anon slips back into the dance with the disease. My sponsor knew his recovery and stayed with it, so he was the best help I could get for this particular problem.

## Learning That I Was Needed

This sponsor wasn't my first sponsor. I had a first sponsor during my initial ten years in the program. However, she found herself in a better relationship (not with an alcoholic) and stopped attending meetings after her solid twenty years in Al-Anon. I was devastated that she stopped showing up. I felt without a person in program. Her leaving the rooms was so upsetting to me because I was a newbie still in love with an alcoholic and trying to live a dream with him. When she gained the courage to divorce her alcoholic after twenty-five years of marriage I was inspired. But I was shocked that she ended up taking him back three years later when he showed up on her porch homeless and desperate. I thought it was impossible for her to forgive the debts he left her with and all his cheating. But she did. She took him back, and within a year… he was right back out! (He quickly found his way into the arms of another woman - of course.) Her second round of courage to kick him back out also inspired me.

So, when my first sponsor stopped going to meetings it left a huge hole that no one could fill. I believed she was needed. Her life experience and program was so valuable to me. Her story was as close to mine as I had found by attending various meetings. I didn't think anyone else could help me the way she could. When her attendance was missing at my main meeting (no attendance is taken at meetings), I felt lost in the program. Seeing someone ahead of me in years, working the steps, surviving divorce, separation, living, making it, and sharing about it was what gave me hope. I believed if she could make it and be happy without the man she loved (the alcoholic), so could I.

I Love an Alcoholic, but Hated The Drinking

After a year without a sponsor, I got the courage to ask another woman to be my sponsor, but she politely said no because she was too busy. I noticed that she had close friends in the program and they seemed complete in their nice, little, close-knit circle. She was also several generations older than I was and her circle consisted of her peers. Often I felt out of place with the age gap at meetings. So, I had to go it alone for a while. Looking for help, I started attending different meetings. A few years later, after I thought she would have been my perfect sponsor, and still feeling rejected by her, she unexpectedly passed away from a rapid form of pancreatic cancer. Sometimes I look back and I can understand why some things might not have been best for me. Obviously, I have completely forgiven her.

## Finding a New Sponsor

I found a new sponsor but I wasn't so sure that my new sponsor was right for me. My current sponsor had several sponsees at the time. I thought he would say no simply because I would be an additional person. He was never married to an alcoholic, but what he did have was knowledge of the Steps and a commitment to recovery and working Step Twelve. That commitment made all the difference. My sponsor was a regular meeting-attender. If my recovering alcoholic grandfather were alive, he would have said that this sponsor was one of the "winners." My AA grandpa always told me to "stick with the winners." I had no idea who the "winners" were but I assumed it was people still in program, having a happy life, and willing to be a sponsor to share the gifts they got.

So, I "stuck with the winners" and my sponsor stuck it out with me. Getting a sponsor was how my recovery advanced. In a sense, I was held accountable to attending meetings and working the Steps but in a very gentle and non-judgmental way (and under no pressure). I began to see where/when I could relapse in my own personal recovery and have Alanonic-slips. For example, dating to me, with codependent tendencies, I was similar to an alcoholic walking into a bar. Temptation was everywhere! I had opportunities to fall into my codependency or

76

choose to work my program. But I didn't have to do it alone. I had a committed sponsor who was dedicated to listening and helping me with my emotional sobriety. I learned so much about the disease of alcoholism through my sponsor. To try to save his son, he had researched alcoholism as a disease and passed down his wisdom to me. It was like having a teacher, coach, mentor, spiritual advisor, and friend all in one but not trying to be any of them in a pushy way. What made the difference was that my sponsor cared. What also made the difference was that my sponsor continued with his recovery evolving and growing. My sponsor kept working the Steps. My sponsor stayed in program. My sponsor was practicing Step Twelve by sponsoring me. My sponsor was paying it forward and inspiring me to do the same. My sponsor was needed. I started to ask myself, "Was I needed too?"

*"Try at least six meetings and then six more, if at any time it's not for you, we will gladly refund your misery."*
*— My Al-Anon Sponsor*

So I said to myself, "Be unstoppable! Continue with your recovery."

## My Take-away Strategy: Unstoppably Continue with My Recovery

I unstoppably continued with my recovery. I kept working the steps. I stayed in the program. I practiced Step Twelve. I was needed, so I paid it forward.

❖ If you would like to read some of my other survival strategies and read FREE excerpts of my other books, please visit my website at: www.GraceWroldson.com

# One of the best feelings in the world is...

One of the best feelings in the world is falling in love.
One of the best feelings in the world is also when you feel like yourself
again
— *after letting someone go.*
One of the best feelings in the world is starting a new beginning.
One of the best feelings in the world is ending something that no
longer serves you.
One of the best feelings in the world is getting new information that
gives you new hope.
One of the best feelings in the world is trusting yourself and believing
in yourself
— *for the first time.*
One of the best feelings in the world is knowing that you had the ability
to love deeply
— *and now turned that love upon yourself.*
One of the best feelings in the world is witnessing your own miracle
— *realizing that you have changed.*
One of the best feelings in the world is when you thought you were
right,
and then everyone finds out that you *were* right.
One of the best feelings in the world is realizing that you survived
childbirth,
and your newborn baby is placed upon your chest
— *and you both fall asleep together.*
One of the best feelings in the world is when you see yourself in
someone else's eyes.
One of the best feelings in the world is twirling your baby's soft, blond
curls in your fingers,
lying beside her while she breathes her first dreams.

Grace W. Wroldson

One of the best feelings in the world is when God puts you in a unique position
— *to truly help someone.*
One of the best feelings in the world is opening your heart to every experience
— *with an open loving heart.*
One of the best feelings in the world is when someone appreciates everything about you,
that someone else took for granted.
One of the best feelings in the world is when someone with a compassionate heart
holds you while you cry and says nothing.
One of the best feelings in the world is when you share a silent, understanding
moment with someone.
One of the best feelings in the world is realizing you're not sad anymore
over something you thought you would never forget.
One of the best feelings in the world is seeing someone with the eyes of compassion
— *that you formerly saw with the eyes of hate.*
One of the best feelings in the world is accomplishing something
— *that you never thought you'd do.*
One of the best feelings in the world is feeling your loneliness dissolve into wholeness.
One of the best feelings in the world is feeling inspired
— *and unstoppable.*
One of the best feelings in the world is when you get to recall and relive a precious feeling.

One of the best feelings in the world is feeling free!

— *Grace W. Wroldson*

# Strategy #5:
# Steadfastly Stay Spiritual,

✓ Stay on a Spiritual Path
✓ Resolutely Realize Your Spiritual Potential
✓ Have a Higher Power

**Adding a Higher Power for Oxygen**

*My one despair worse than, "God, I ruined my life with this drinker!" was,*
*"God, I ruined my life with this drinker, again!"*
— *Grace W. Wroldson*

**Question:** Where do I get the love that the alcoholic doesn't/won't/can't provide?
**Answer:** A Higher Power.

## My Miracle

Back in my relationship days, actively loving an active alcoholic, it never occurred to me to ask for a miracle for myself. I was continually asking for the miracle for him, you know the one that would change him and get him to quit drinking - so I could be happy. In my recovery, I had to learn to ask for a miracle for me. I had to stay spiritual and keep on the spiritual path, which was essentially a path of truth that led to my many insights, awarenesses, and awakenings.

He was struggling with alcoholism, I was struggling with him (and my love-sick, codependent self) so I desperately needed a miracle. In my first book, *So You Love an… Alcoholic?: Lessons for a Codependent,* I explained my path to a spirituality that spoke to me. Once I started on the spiritual path, I learned that I needed to stay on the path. I needed to continue my spiritual growth, strengthen my spiritual muscles, do my spiritual exercises, and realize my spiritual potential.

**My First Experience of a Higher Power**

At age sixteen, just before entering the alcoholic relationship, I was suicidal. I'm not sure I actually wanted to kill myself, it was more like I just wanted to die. Nobody knew. It was my secret. I never shared about it with anyone. It lasted a few days. I remember being alone locked-up in my bedroom, emotionally abandoned by my emotionally unavailable parents, and having a deep dark night of the soul. I was alone. I felt alone. I reached a place where I felt like there was no hope for me. My only problem with following through on suicide was how to do it painlessly because I had suffered so much pain in my life, I couldn't handle any more (even if it was to permanently end the pain I was in).

Desperate for a painless way to end my life, lying on my bedroom floor, rolling in this soul sickness, I happened glanced over at my nightstand. A book stood out to me. I had collected it years ago, based on its cover, but never read it. I knew that it had something to do with God. I didn't believe in God so it never was opened. The word God was so foreign to me and I couldn't translate what I thought was an ancient, outdated idea.

It was upon opening the book that I had my first spiritual awakening at age sixteen. Someone's life-saving red pen crossed out every word God and replaced it with the re-written word of "Love." It was from there that my suicidal thoughts stopped. It only took two paragraphs of that book, (edited in red) and I was saved. I believed in the power of "Love" because I could feel love and see love everywhere in my life with my loving grandparents. So the person's edited translation for me worked. That was my first experience of being a spiritual being. How did I forget that profound moment after all these years? Do we all have moments like that, that we forget?

**Reaching Outside of Myself for Help**

Afterwards, after fifteen years in an alcoholic relationship, trying to survive the withdrawal of my addiction to loving him and the grief of losing all my dreams, I had to reach outside of myself for help again because inside I was a mess. I came to believe in a personal Higher Power through the Twelve-Step Group of Al-Anon. I didn't realize at the time that both the drinker and I were suffering a spiritual dilemma living life without a Higher Power. In order to stay spiritual, in order to stay on a spiritual path, I asked myself often, "How could a Higher Power help?"

I began to wonder: What is a miracle? Is it when God bends the fabric of space and time to accomplish something that seems impossible? Or could it be something simpler?

Before studying what a miracle actually was, I didn't know that a miracle can be defined as simply a shift in perception, out of fear, and into a state seeing everything with the eyes of love and gratitude. If that was the definition of a miracle, I could certainly control some of my perceptions now. I had enough recovery and time in the Twelve-Step program to identify when I was thinking negatively about my dilemma with the alcoholic. I had learned what were my patterns and bad habits. My negativity, anxiety, and low self-worth was just as destructive as alcohol was to the alcoholic. I was addicted to my own pain. I was addicted to loving him. I needed a miracle.

## The Danger in Waiting for Someone Else's Miracle

If I only believed that the true definition of a miracle was when God bent the laws of the Universe in a particular situation, then I was mistakenly waiting on just one thing to happen for me to be happy. When I believed that a miracle was ONLY that... I was engaging my "expectation problem." I expected things and got disappointed as a result.

For years, I was expecting a DUI or OUI to wake the drinker up and so finally, at long last he would get help in AA. But that's just not what happened. He didn't get that miracle. However, I stayed in program and got my miracle. I shifted my attention to acts of self-love and listened (and followed) my own soul out of the painful relationship. I learned that a miracle can have many definitions. However, God bent the laws of nature for me a few times after I decided to follow a Power Greater than myself. Because I began to see those miracles.

## Without a Higher Power

Until having a Higher Power, until this happened, until I was willing to believe, until I came to believe; I just kept trying all my old tricks, you know the ones that never worked, but kept me thinking might work - this time! Like many people, things had to get really bad before I would open the door and let a notion of a Higher Power in. Yet, oftentimes the change I was really looking for was inside my head the whole time.

In recovery I was learning how valuable keeping an open mind is, I continued to keep a space open for a Higher Power to bend Universal Laws on my behalf and help the alcoholic reach sobriety and AA recovery. Raising a child with an active alcoholic was concerning, and I had many reasons for concern in this situation. I prayed for deliverance. I prayed that my child would get the gift of having a sober father. I prayed that the alcoholic would reach AA. But I looked for my miracles, instead of just hoping for his.

## Being Able to Breathe

Before recovery, I didn't know that whatever I was mentally obsessed with, I instantly made my Higher Power. I certainly was obsessed with the alcoholic. So by default, I mistakenly made him a Power Greater than me. By doing this I inadvertently allowed my life to be misdirected, troubled, and confused. Giving over my power to the relationship made me feel like my life was not my own. One of the worst consequences of giving over my power to the alcoholic relationship was that I became physically ill. It was like I had no oxygen. Being in a state of constant anxiety and panic does something to one's oxygen supply - for sure. And before having a Higher Power I didn't have a prayer. When my life became unmanageable, I learned to look beyond myself for answers— to a Higher Power. Having a Higher

Power was a source of hope. I had to believe in a Source of healing. Before I had a Higher Power, I was asking "What do I need a Higher Power for?" At my bottom, I learned what I needed it for.

I needed a Higher Power to humble me and to get through the hard stuff. There were limits to what I could achieve without help. Self-help could only accomplish so much. By myself, I could only do what was humanly possible. By accepting my limitations I availed myself of the unlimited possibilities of a Higher Power. This became a powerful partnership with a Power greater than myself. It helped me let go of all that stood in my way of a happy life. A program friend said, "We don't make changes by ourselves. We use the Holy Spirit and we get the help of God." I appreciated her insistence on having a Higher Powered life. I decided that if I am going to center my life around anything it would be a loving source of goodness and love and not the alcoholic.

## A Spiritual Bypass

In my first book, _So You Love an… Alcoholic?,_ I explained how I had to get past my own disbelief. I couldn't let vocabulary hold me back from having a Higher Power. I had to go around myself (cross off the word God in red) and call it "Love." Every time someone mentioned God, I reworded it in my mind to the word "Love." This is how I overcame the language barrier that I had. I was standing in my own way of Higher Help. I needed a spiritual bypass around my own closed mind.

To survive, I had to stop allowing vocabulary to hold me back from adding a Higher Power into my life. Some called it God, Love, The Great Spirit, Spirit, Source, or The Universe. I didn't know what to call my Higher Power. Whatever I chose to call the "sustaining infinite" that day, I decided not to allow the name to get in my way of finding it and using its power and peace to renew my life. **Having a Higher Power was my highest strategy.**

I made a connection to something greater than me when I connected to the idea of a Higher Power. At first it was the feeling of Love, but eventually I was able to call that God. I had to get myself comfortable to surrender into this high idea. For a long time I needed to replace the word God with Love to be comfortable believing. I also made my Twelve-Step recovery group a type of Higher Power surrogate until I was completely comfortable and content. I did whatever it took.

The truth was that my recovery could only get me so far (with a reliance solely on myself). My will-power could only do so much before its continual usage made me feel drained. Only when I found relief in a Higher Power could I continue onto a spiritual awakening and have a sustaining recovery. I had to ask myself, what type of recovery did I want to have? The kind that lasts? Well if so, was I willing to ask for this high powered help?

## Being a "Believer"

I began to believe that a Higher Power could and already did provide for me in ways that man and the material world could never provide. It was really important in my recovery to make peace with the fact that I was not the sole driving power of the world, not even my own world. This humbled me. It also took the world off my shoulders. I embraced this with the knowledge that I could not control everything. I did not have the total say in what, how, and when all things, could, would, and do happen. I humbled myself with that truth often. These desires and cravings to control came from the fact that I was in a totally uncontrollable situation with the alcoholic.

## Acknowledging Two Wills at Work, Co-creating My Universe

I had to acknowledge that besides my will there was another will at work in my life. On one hand there was my will and on the other was my Higher Power's will. I believed that this was a co-created world that I was living in. I believed that we were both working in my life to create things. I learned to like sharing the job.

I often saw that my Higher Power would give and take away. I had to learn to let go of what my Higher Power took away that no longer served me. The "taking away" was sometimes my most difficult things to accept. But how could my Higher Power give me anything new without first removing things? I learned to be as thankful for the gifts as the losses. I learned that this was part of life and not personal (even if it felt personal and I took it personal).

I had to learn to use what my Higher Power had given me and then make the best of it. I also had to learn from what my Higher Power put on my path and grow from it. This was me embracing life, the lessons, and change. This was stepping out of my internal resistance to how things are - and letting things be as they are. I was acquiring higher powers. These powers showed up in the form of grace and quiet acceptance.

Once I had a solid belief and faith in a Higher Power, then I became miles ahead on the recovery road with a power source who would never let me down. I notice how some people found the suggestion of having a Higher Power a real roadblock in recovery. Their resistance was so strong to believe in something that could not be seen or proved. I saw that they could not get out of their own way on this subject and it held them back from full immersion into the Steps of the program. I decided to give a Higher Power a try or at least open my mind to the idea. I didn't want to be stuck on the same spot on the road. **Oftentimes, I was waiting on a Higher Power, and found out that my Higher Power was waiting on me.**

## How I Got In Touch With A Power Greater Than Myself

I discovered the much needed help available in the form of a Higher Power's assistance and peace. I learned to ask for both. How did I get in touch with this Higher Power? I learned to pray. Prayer was a simple tool that that I used to call on the graces of God. My prayers started out as just journal entries to my Higher Power. I had to remember to pray for myself first, just like the instructions on a plane trip's emergency plan —to put on your oxygen mask first. I had to be able to breathe to survive this mess. Letters to God became lifesavers.

I Love an Alcoholic, but Hated The Drinking

Here was my most basic prayer, "Dear God, please help me."

I chose to stay on a spiritual path and stay spiritual and continue my journey in recovery. Miracle after miracle began to happen. And I began to see them. I miraculously survived a childbirth experience that should have killed me. My child survived a pregnancy that should have aborted her. I survived years of court custody battles that should have taken my child away from me. I survived two major abdominal surgeries in one year and an infection that was going to kill me if an angel (in the form of a surgeon with powers of intuition and experience) didn't show up at the last minute. Back when I was sixteen, I survived suicidal thoughts by having a Higher Power show up in a book. And I never had those thoughts again.

After surviving all these things, I wanted to be used by a Higher Power for great things. I began realizing my spiritual potential. I was realizing my spiritual potential with every prayer and trust in a power greater than me. With a Power Greater than myself I was able to stay spiritually strong. I stayed spiritually strong by practicing several spiritual exercises, one of which was making it to meetings and connecting to the spiritual grid of recovery (often). My spiritual muscles grew. I began to ask myself, "Am I able to see my miracles?" I certainly was experiencing a miracle life make-over. I saw my life change.

So I told myself, "Be Steadfast. Stay Spiritual!"

## My Take-a-way Strategy: Steadfastly Stay Spiritual

I steadfastly stayed spiritual throughout my recovery. I resolutely realized my spiritual potential by staying on a spiritual path. I connected with my loving, wise, and patient Higher Power. I reminded myself to breathe and pray— *daily*.

❖ If you would like to read some of my other survival strategies and read FREE excerpts of my other books, please visit my website at: www.GraceWroldson.com

# Strategy #6:
# Audaciously Question Everything,

## Including Yourself

✓ Live in "The Mystery"
✓ Ask Yourself Powerful Questions to Make a Shift

*"Be patient toward all that is unsolved in your heart and try to love the questions themselves, like locked rooms and like books that are now written in a very foreign tongue. Do not now seek the answers, which cannot be given you because you would not be able to live them. And the point is, to live everything. Live the questions now. Perhaps you will then gradually, without noticing it, live along some distant day into the answer."*

— *Rainer Maria Rilke*

**Questions for the Soul**

**I never stopped to knock and ask myself, "Why was I with an alcoholic?"**

## *Opening the Door to My Psyche*

I began to question everything. As I became healthier, I questioned everyone who thought they had simple answers to cure an alcoholic relationship. More importantly, I finally questioned myself. What was I doing loving him (so much) and not loving myself (at all)? In order to get better answers, I had to ask better questions. So, I stopped asking why does the alcoholic drink and why doesn't he stop. Instead, I asked, "What am I doing with him?"

I Love an Alcoholic, but Hated The Drinking

It's scary for me to realize that before a decade of recovery, I thought I had all the answers. Was I always right? No. I was self-righteous, believing that the alcoholic was the only person with a problem. In my second decade of recovery, I woke up and realized that I was choosing this life of disrespect. When I saw my part in my problems, I wandered around clueless and keyless and felt as though I didn't know anything. I finally began to question myself. That is when the door of my mind opened. **Questions are powerful openings to the psyche.**

*"If you live the questions, life will move you into the answers."*
— *Deepak Chopra*

In the first ten years of recovery, I had convinced myself that I had my "shit together." After all, I told myself, I have good grades, a steady job, and life figured out. I had pursued a safe degree in college, worked hard at three different jobs, and picked a man that I thought was the best person to live life with, love, marry, have a family with, and own a home together. In my blind state of ignorance, I thought, after all, he built houses for a living, and one of the things that I really wanted in life was a home. I never took the time to ask myself why having a house was that serious of a life goal to me. If I had asked myself that question, I might have uncovered that I didn't feel like I had a home growing up (where I felt I belonged and with some feeling of ownership). If I had known what my specific childhood traumas were, and what I was trying to avoid feeling again, I might not have made so many subconscious choices. I could have chosen differently, as I do today.

*"Most misunderstandings in the world could be avoided if people would simply take the time to ask, "What else could this mean?"*
— *Shannon L. Alder*

## Questions To Others

I thought I had all the answers in my 20's. What I had were a bunch of closed, judgmental doors in my mind. I had self-righteousness. When I started self-help and started learning how to change my life, I discovered that questions opened the door to possibilities. Whereas answers shut doors and stopped any further entry. Questions went right to the soul because my mind couldn't conjure up a quick answer to deep questioning. So, I learned to ask questions directed to my soul.

In a life coaching training program that I completed, we students were not taught how to answer other people's problems for their life, rather we were taught how to ask powerful questions so our coaching client would look inward. Young and naive, I mistakenly thought life coaching was lecturing others on how to get their life right, like I often lectured the alcoholic. I spent hours and years trying to explain to him why drinking was bad for his health. He learned to block out all my unsolicited advice regarding his drinking.

My pre-recovery, sick self was surprised to hear that I had to mostly listen and let my coaching clients talk. This was uncomfortable for me because I still had unresolved codependent control issues and I wanted to help by fixing. I didn't know that the best gift I could give someone is to witness their journey. I learned that we all just need a loving witness in our lives. Someone who sees our journey and *really* sees us can be the best gift of all (that's where a good sponsor comes in). Before this eye-opening life coaching training, I was trying to give people answers for their life problems but they weren't my problems to begin with. So none of my answers worked (and they were unwanted).

## Watching Out For "Know-it-alls"

In an alcoholic relationship, to protect myself from others, I learned to stay away from Know-it-alls because they just thought they knew it all —and didn't listen. But most importantly, I also had to watch out for the Know-it-all, in me. How could I have answers for another person's soul? How humbling it was to discover that I didn't have the answers for anyone else nor myself (at that time). Instead I had questions I needed to ask myself like, "Why was I with an alcoholic?" I further asked, "What made me take him back after the breakups?" Before my maturity developed, before I understood the natural world better, I didn't understand the concept of how nature filled voids, nor how *my* nature was filling *my* voids. Asking these questions woke me up to the holes I had within. Holes that I could fill with my Higher Power's help.

## Skillful Listening Leads To Simple Questions

When I completed that training, I was attentively listening for the question that I could suggest that my life coaching clients might ask themselves. I took a more humble role. I realized that they had to come up with their own answers from within themselves and their souls. My timing was everything. I found that clients had to be all "talked-out" before I could ask a question. Any success I had with clients depended on my ability to listen fully and find the most powerful questions and give those questions as a gift. The questions I offered my clients proved to be more powerful than any advice or suggestion I could ever come up with. It confirmed to me that questions are truly powerful. Questions helped my clients shift from the problem into their solution. Questions opened the door to their minds. Questions opened them up to their inner resources. I learned first-hand what neuroscientists have long known, we are not accessing or using all of our brain. I only later realized that I needed to access this powerful tool for myself. I had to ask myself powerful questions. **Questions opened me up to my Inner Resources.**

*"To ask the 'right' question is far more important than to receive the answer. The solution of a problem lies in the understanding of the problem; the answer is not outside the problem, it is in the problem."*
— *Jiddu Krishnamurti, The Flight of the Eagle*

Grace W. Wroldson

## Questions from My Sponsor

I also found this principle to be true for me. (The principal of asking questions vs. giving answers to create a shift into solutions that work.) The best things that my sponsor in the Al-Anon program ever said to me were in the form of interjected questions - at just the right moment. This took great skill, especially to get a word in edgewise to my sometimes lengthy, non-stop, hours of talking on the phone about my codependent issues. All cleverly disguised with my complaining about the alcoholic. Sometimes, when I think back on ten years of venting about the alcoholic, I can't believe a sponsor could be so patient listening to me for hours (letting me talk, talk, talk). My sponsor then would ask just one simple question. My sponsor's patience with my process made me realize that sponsorship was definitely a role similar to that of a spiritual director. My sponsor removed himself from my story and saw it from a higher perspective. This was valuable. Sometimes my sponsor would ask, "How is that working out for you?" or "Why are you choosing that?" Those were empowering questions because it woke me up to realizing that I had choices. Sometimes my sponsor would ask, "What about your Higher Power?" "Where is your Higher Power in all of this?" And I would get stopped in my tracks from walking further into the sinking sand trap of self-pity (a door that leads *only* downwards). With those powerful questions, doors of my mind would swing wide open.

*"He explained to me with great insistence that every question possessed a power that did not lie in the answer."*
— *Elie Wiesel, Night*

## Questions From Others

When I was a single parent and my child needed early intervention, as well as other support services, someone asked me a question that I will never forget. I was on an intake interview call with a highly sought-after family therapist, who had a full schedule (and wasn't taking new clients), but had a special place in his heart for three-year-olds and was willing to help us. He asked me on the phone, before setting up any sessions, "How responsible do you feel as a parent that your child has needs and issues?" I answered immediately with; "Totally responsible!" He then asked me about what percent do I consider myself responsible. He asked; "Is it 80% or 90% responsible for your child's problems?" I replied, "It's more like 115%. Is that an option?"

I heard myself say this and immediately realized how ridiculous it sounded. It shocked me to know that I was solely blaming myself for having a child with an alcoholic. I was blaming myself for my child's struggles - every single one. I was being overly responsible —again. But I felt that I was taking all the responsibility because the alcoholic would take none. I took on all the problems because I believed I was smarter and ought to have known better than to have a child with that man, under those circumstances. I blamed myself. That powerful question he asked at the beginning of our sessions revealed so much, about me, to him. I wasn't being reasonable by taking total responsibility. I was being an anxious, guilty parent. The question helped me see that I was blaming myself for my child's struggles. It helped me recognize that it's absurd to take on that much responsibility when there are hundreds of other factors affecting my child's life. For example, an alcoholic father who wasn't helping us because his alcoholism held him back. What about him? What about his percentage of parenting he was not able to do? Even so, I had stopped blaming the alcoholic because I observed that he wouldn't/couldn't help in his state. I needed a balanced perspective on who/what was responsible. I had to stop blaming myself.

**Meetings With Myself**

I then found the best door to opening myself up to a better life. I learned to question myself (daily). I would create meetings with myself in the mornings or when I was in a codependent crisis. I still went to face-to-face recovery meetings because they were essential to my

# Grace W. Wroldson

practice of the Twelve Steps. I also found that reading The Steps in the morning, and then reading The ACA Promises at night were a like a mini-meeting that I needed to hold with myself. I also held these mini-meetings with myself by searching the back of my recovery books on a topic and reading all the pages available. This was also a suggestion by my sponsor. He led me to this after asking me (in the form of a question) about my ability to create self-solutions and look for resources within my recovery resources. Frantically, I would call my sponsor with a new/next alcoholic-codependent crises and my sponsor would ask: "Well, where is your recovery on this issue?" "Have you looked it up?"

*"Courage doesn't happen when you have all the answers. It happens when you are ready to face the questions you have been avoiding your whole life."*
*— Shannon L. Alder*

## Questioning Myself

By asking myself questions, I was acknowledging that I might not always be right. I questioned myself when I caught myself assuming something or adamantly thinking that I knew what was best. I learned that sometimes the most important thing to say in life was, "I don't know," and ask, "What else is possible?" I found that asking myself questions was one of the most important ways I changed my codependently stuck mindset. Instead of sticking with the thought that my alcoholic was never going to find AA or sobriety (an answer I assigned him over my years of frustration), I learned to stop coming up with answers for him and others. I learned to question myself and ask, "What about me?" "Where is my focus?" "Right now, am I being part of the problem or part of the solution?"

### My Lesson:

✓ Question Everything,
✓ Including Myself

95

## Living In "The Mystery," Finding The Key

*"There are years that ask questions and years that answer."*
— *Zora Neale Hurston*

I found a key to life that has helped me open doors. The key is learning how to ask questions. Another key came from living in "the question." I had to learn to hold the question in my mind but not grasp at the answer. As a codependent, control freak, I had a hard time living in the unknown. One spiritual master I studied under taught about living "in the mystery" as a form of mastery with life. She described a cycle of change and taught us that we had to go through "mystery times" when one part of our life ends and before our life took a new form. She made the mystery times of life sound like a beautiful phase of magic and possibility. When I adopted her thinking, I found "The Mystery" to indeed have a magical quality that held open doors for me. A mystery time was like being in a room surrounded by doors that were all wide open to me. But I didn't have to commit to any entry or path, I just had to observe, wait and "live in the mystery." I would serenely sit and patiently let my soul select new entryways back into my life. When I made a choice, I did it with new questions. Even though I was choosing a door to go through (picking an answer) that felt right on all levels (and inside and outside). I learned to continue to walk with questions as I moved forward. I walked with the soul-searching questions. Sometimes I asked questions directed at my Higher Power. For example, "What is all this for?" or "Where will this take me?"

### Asking My Higher Power

Before recovery, I was like an angry child who didn't know better. Demanding from a Higher Power and the Universe something lesser in the name of something better. I wanted my relationship with the alcoholic. And it would have been very sad if I got it.

As I became more spiritual, I questioned my Higher Power from a stronger sense of self and soul. I asked for daily directions and directives. Those powerful questions to a powerful Power led me to walk through double-wide doors. They turned out to be the best questions to ask. So, I learned to ask, wait, and listen. I asked, "What is my Higher Power's will for me, right now?"

And I told myself, "Be audacious!"

*"In the past, I always used to be looking for answers. Today, I know there are only questions."*
— *Sarah Brightman*

## My Take-a-way Strategy: Audaciously Question Everything, Including Myself

I audaciously questioned everything, including my own thoughts, beliefs, and actions. I questioned my motives for everything. I learned to live in the mystery regularly and comfortably. I was able to open and unlock the door to my psyche with questions. I learned to ask questions directed to my soul so that I could navigate myself in my truest, most authentic direction. I learned to ask a power greater than me for help and daily direction. My life took on more meaning. My life became higher powered with higher questions.

### Important Questions I asked myself:

➤ What about me? (especially helpful when with an alcoholic)
➤ What's my motive? (for doing, wanting, asking everything)

❖ If you would like to read some of my other survival strategies and read FREE excerpts of my other books, please visit my website at: www.GraceWroldson.com

# Strategy #7:
# Aggressively Pinpoint Your Patterns

✓ Learn from Your Own History

✓ Recognize When You Hurt Yourself with Relationships

*"Perhaps we can recognize our way out of patterns rather than repeating our way out of them."*
— *Patti Digh, Life Is a Verb: 37 Days to Wake Up, Be Mindful, and Live Intentionally*

**I asked myself, "What were my patterns?"**

## *Driving Old Roads*

In recovery, I watched people perpetuate their problems with patterns. (Say that 5 times fast!) Me? My patterns were people-problems. I had a long history of harmful behavior (towards myself) involving people, especially the alcoholic. I had so many patterns that I didn't recognize in myself, yet I was constantly complaining about how the alcoholic was doing the same things over and over. Obsession with the alcoholic would hit me like a hurricane. I talked about how I noticed he seemed to have a cycle of chaos that he continued with, year after year, that I could almost set my calendar to. Unfortunately, complaining was one of my patterns! I, myself, had cycles of dysfunction and self-destruction too. My patterns were playing out with people. I just didn't see them at first. They were old, dirt roads in my mind and they were bumpy and well worn. And I got bounced around on every bump, so to speak.

*Until you are willing to learn the lessons, pay attention to details, and become patient with yourself, you will keep repeating the same patterns over and over again.*

# I Love an Alcoholic, but Hated The Drinking

*— Kemi Sogunle*

I had to recognize when I was hurting myself with relationships. I also had to recognize that I had rights in those relationships. I needed to come to recognize respect as much as disrespect, so I could stay away from toxically-filled, negative-minded people and make healthier friends. This required me to have and hold boundaries. This required my boundaries to actually function. This required boundaries with myself, not just the alcoholic.

## Identifying The Patterns of My Love Trajectory

My patterns were actually an energy pattern. Allowing patterns to determine my fate was like being on autopilot or cruise control on a windy dirt road. I lost count of how many times I took the alcoholic back after our numerous breakups. My pattern was agreeing to get back into the alcoholic relationship, over and over (with the same hope). My pattern was sliding back into dysfunctional codependency and slipping back into focusing on him again. My pattern was giving into my pride. Unfortunately, I often allowed my pride to determine my destiny. But when I figured this out, what I tried to do was intercept these patterns of mine. I had to interject new energy (do something new and different) to determine a new destiny, rather than play out my fate. Detouring myself around my autopiloted-self was how I paved new roads in my life and created a new future. I took myself off of cruise control and I learned to steer myself better. I was sick of watching my history repeat itself.

*"If we experience any failures or setbacks, we do not forget them because they offend our self-esteem. Instead we reflect on them deeply, trying to figure out what went wrong and discern whether there are any patterns to our mistakes."*

*— Robert Greene, Mastery*

## Identifying The Problem

Before recovery, I thought that alcohol, in its liquid form, was my alcoholic's *only* problem. Before recovery, I also thought his alcohol was *my* only problem, too. What I didn't see and what I didn't know was that the alcohol use/abuse was only one symptom pointing to our suffering. I had suffered things that I didn't acknowledge in my life, and these sufferings were my driving factors into a relationship with him. I had no idea what the driving factors were that drove the alcoholic to drink. All I knew was that I was not his reason for drinking —no matter what he claimed. There was heavy traffic inside us of our past traumas. Our internal highways were congested. There were complex problems within each of us that neither one of us created, but came from our childhoods and conditioning. Our internal driving factors were there before we ended up in a relationship together. And our problems were there after we ended the relationship.

*"What we call chaos is just patterns we haven't recognized. What we call random is just patterns we can't decipher."*

*— Chuck Palahniuk*

## Identifying The Parts

The problem came down to finding the parts of myself that were my "problem-parts." Seeing my patterns was how I could see my subconscious shaping my life. There were patterns to his illness, and there were patterns to mine. Identifying these were like solving a mystery within me. **If I wanted to know what was buried in the dark alleyways of my subconscious, all I had to do was look at my patterns.** They were the one-way signs pointing to my pain. I was self-righteous when I thought that he was the one with all the problems. I had to identify my own unhealthy patterns. I had my own blind-spots.

When I began serious inner-work in Al-Anon and ACOA, I found a small wounded child inside of me. I found parts that were traumatized and unhealed. I had to find these parts and look in detail at the patterns that they played out in my life. Some of these parts of me couldn't handle making a mistake so they would push me and pull me in different directions, until I was consumed by work and practically a workaholic. Some of these parts of me couldn't handle loss, and so, I hung on to jobs and partners, unable to let go, even for my own good.

101

Yet, I was made up of parts that were dysfunctional and parts that were functional. To steer myself, I had to find ways to intercept the fear-based parts with awareness and make sure those parts were not making my decisions for me. I had to practice intercepting myself when I was going into reaction mode and not responding from a mature, solid sense of self. I found ways to stop myself at stop signs I commissioned for myself. Other times, I would imagine holding up an actual STOP sign. This was a huge effort that took years of practicing recovery behaviors and years of phone calls to program friends. I was designed by my childhood so, naturally I had patterns, parts, and problems to heal and overcome.

## My Lesson:

✓ Pinpoint my patterns
✓ Learn from my own history

## Healthy Patterns And Unhealthy Patterns

*"Even when something is not your fault, toxic blame has no place in your life. Focus on your own empowerment and healing."*
— *Bryant McGill, Simple Reminders: Inspiration for Living Your Best Life*

After focusing on my problem patterns for way too long, I realized that I had good patterns of behavior that led to good things, too. I noticed that when I was not in an alcoholic relationship, playing out my sickness with his, I thrived. My life flourished when I was single and able to focus on myself and fill my life with activities that I loved. I didn't have his alcoholism undermining me, and I didn't have my codependency trying to control him (undermining me). I discovered that as much as I needed to learn from my history of repeating unhealthy patterns, I could learn from the healthy patterns in my life and replicate those. This was a positive way I encouraged myself to steer clear of future alcoholic relationships. This was how I identified my inner love-addict tendencies. This is how I learned to savor the years of my life when I wasn't being an active codependent. I could look back over my history and see things that I couldn't see in the moment. I began to get into healthy energy patterns.

*"Being broken isn't the worst thing. We can be mended and put together again..."*
— *Anna White, Mended: Thoughts on Life, Love, and Leaps of Faith*

## My Goal, My Progression

My goal was not just pinpointing my dysfunctional patterns and intercepting them, it was also about creating new behaviors with new patterns. I pinpointed my unhealthy tendencies and balanced it with noticing beneficial ones. Then, my healing had to continue with channeling new patterns of thinking. For example, when I would start to feel lonely, instead of reaching for the alcoholic or a new relationship, I reached for a relationship with myself and my Higher Power. I reached for a pen and paper, or a book with a positive message, or a meeting with a healthy recovery friend. I learned to do something different and that led to different results.

I also became good at recognizing when I would get side-tracked and be self-destructive in my habits or thoughts (or both), by being consciously aware of myself. When relationship sugar cravings came on, I was prepared to meet them with a more matured mind. Doing this mindfulness practice - of pinpointing my patterns - helped me recognize that I had some solutions within myself. This helped me see some of myself as my problem, that way I could see myself as the solution. When I looked for the pattern, I also stopped taking things so personally. That too was the pattern I needed to look at! Sadly, I noted that I had a pattern of perpetual pain.

*"Make your pain productive and you can transform tragedy into triumph."*
— *Jaeda DeWalt*

## Recognizing When I Hurt Myself With Relationships

I Love an Alcoholic, but Hated The Drinking

One of my biggest problems as a constantly, craving codependent woman was facing my loneliness. Without a relationship, I would get sick with loneliness. I became lonely often with my inner love-addict at the wheel, and it drove me on all kinds of seek and supply missions. I found many worse relationships to get into than an alcoholic one, when I was in a desperate, lonely state. So, I took classes and workshops trying to solve this loneliness problem, because my pattern was to be alone (without a romantic relationship) as self-punishment for the last failed relationship, only to become so lonely that I would take anyone who provided me attention because it was a relief from that loneliness. It was a form of starving myself. This was a pattern I wanted to intercept. I tried to master the art of aloneness, but a wise teacher said that I ought to practice the art of wholeness instead. I asked myself, "How can I break this pattern?" "How do I become whole?" As a recovering love-addict and codependent, the irony was that I certainly was not going to become whole with someone else. I asked myself a very powerful question, "What if I am already whole?" After my sponsor asked me, "Why do you believe that you are not whole?"

*"If we want to grow, the way to break a pattern of negativity is to face anything negative with love."*
*— Molly Friedenfeld, The Book of Simple Human Truths*

So I said to myself, "Be aggressive! Learn from my own history."

## My Take-a-way: Aggressively Pinpoint My Patterns

I aggressively pinpointed my patterns and learned from my own history. I recognized when I was hurting myself with relationships and I stopped driving down those old roads. I paved new highways in my mind towards a smoother, better future.

❖ If you would like to read some of my other survival strategies and read FREE excerpts of my other books, please visit my website at: www.GraceWroldson.com

# Strategy #8:
# Respectfully Learn from Others

✓ Listen and Learn
✓ Get Some Help

*"We learn from each other. We learn from others' mistakes, from their experience, their wisdom. It makes it easier for us to come to better decisions in our own lives."*
— *Adrian Grenier*

**Wisdom is Expensive**

*Messy Stories and Situations*

**I asked myself, "Why is it that I can see myself in others?"**

Twenty years in, I was tired of paying "the price." Having and raising a child with an alcoholic was messy. It was also costly. Hundreds of times we were in and out of court and it cost hundreds of dollars. I would sit on the waiting benches in court and watched other couples (like us) go in ahead of us and listened to their stories. Their lot sounded strangely similar and I could identify. I knew the huge cost of the lawyers they were retaining. It was nothing I could ever afford but I know they hired the best army their money could afford for the war. Within minutes, after hearing a summary of their story, I knew who the "players" were. After each party spoke, after each ruling of a judge, I had learned something I didn't know. After each phone call with my affordable attorney, I also learned things I didn't know. The battlefield that would have been in my home had now entered the courts. The psychic, emotional, and mental costs that would have been in my home were also now in the courts.

I was no longer in an alcoholic relationship but yet I was. I was on the other side— outside of the relationship— so I could see more clearly. My heart was no longer hurting and pulling my head around with decisions. I was able to sit and observe. Ahead of me in court would be a man or a woman fearing for their child (or children) and on the other side (the other party) would be trying to get their parenting rights reestablished after either 1. messing up with drugs or alcohol or 2. being missing from parenting altogether 3. being cut out 4. not being cooperative. There were numerous variations of what I call a mess. And it seemed that the ones that had alcoholism or addiction involved were the messiest. Unfortunately, I was one of those cases. I could see myself in others.

**Being Affected**

I sat in court year after year learning because we went to court year after year. I also sat in hundreds, more like thousands, of recovery meetings and listened to others being affected. It had an impact on me to hear their stories of mistakes, loss, coping, and survival. There is an estimate that perhaps has no factual or statistical current data to back it up; in general seven people are affected by the disease of alcoholism. However, due to my personal experience, I extrapolate this further. If those original, affected seven are walking around affecting others then there are many people more to add in the "affected column." It's like we are all insane from this insanity. What a big mess we are all in together from the alcoholic-codependent relationship! And then there are the children. Thankfully, by practicing recovery in the Twelve Step groups, I got the opportunity to stop the second round of people being affected *by me*. And that's what my recovery focused on. I stopped how expensive my life would be to me and my child because I got help.

Grace W. Wroldson

# Recovery For/From Everything

My sponsor told me that when he entered Al-Anon, he had people tell him to replace the word alcoholic with anything or any situation they were struggling with. He said that when we are desperate enough (and open minded enough) we are able to learn. He believed that we got into recovery exactly on time, right when we needed it. So I respectfully, listened and learned about situations that I wasn't involved in (at the time) as people shared their problems and pain in meetings. I couldn't relate to their issues with houses because I didn't have a home. I couldn't relate to their trouble with children because I didn't have a child at the time. I couldn't relate to so many things but I learned. I learned what a situation could be like and what it could do to a person like me --because I could relate to them as a person fighting these fights in these particular battles on this complicated battlefield. I gained wisdom on topics that saved me money in the long run because by being aware I avoided so much more. I knew that war cost more than just money. It was expensive in other ways, too.

## Attending Meetings to Make It

Meetings were huge investments with huge returns. I invested in attending meetings several times a week. I learned not to have a second child with an active alcoholic or what the consequences would possibly be. I learned to let go of the dream and the man; or lose. I learned not to marry an active alcoholic or mix my finances with him or what the consequences could amount to. I learned not to try to co-parent with someone toxic and learned to keep intermediaries and good personal boundaries in place— always. I learned how to handle myself with all my tendencies to worry, project, fear, and dread. I learned by listening so I didn't have to make the same costly mistakes. After each person shared in a meeting, I would ask myself, "What did you just learn?" **I learned to learn what others were learning.** And that changed the trajectory of my life and court case. My child's first seven years were in a non-alcoholic home receiving early intervention, therapy, and activities with a regular schedule that limited contact but provided her consistency and stability. She was "immunized by my recovery" as my sponsor suggested. This was definitely a "vaccine" I believed in.

People in my situation were paying hundreds of thousands of dollars to unaffordable attorneys and going broke. One woman in a similar situation was taking out school loans for her nursing program and using them to pay for a divorce attorney. Another man had paid an attorney the cost of three houses to try to get to see his four children, who in the end wanted nothing to do with him as adults. People in my situation were taking the alcoholic back with false hope and ruining their credibility in the courts when it came to custody of children. Judges were ruling on 50/50 custody for partners who broke up and got back together. People in my situation were freaking out with fear rather than being calm and centered. Judges were picking up on the emotional and mental instability of parents. People in my situation were trying to do things all on their own and maintain some semblance of pride while I had learned to ask for help and humble myself. Judges were not condoning parents who tried to live outside of their means yet claim poverty when providing financial statements to the court. People in my situation were usually still so focused on the alcoholic changing while I was focused on moving on and changing myself. My case was never about waiting for my ex to get better like some other cases were because I wasn't waiting for that anymore. However, even though I had the right focus, that's where I met my human limitations.

Among my limitations was the fact that I could not cure myself with simple self-help. Nevermind the alcoholic, I had achieved the humility that was necessary for my change to take place. Every time I tried self-help on my own, my human side was in charge and messed things up. I learned to sit and listen. I learned to ask for a Higher Power's help. I absorbed the moral of the story from each court case ahead of me and each person who shared at a recovery meeting. These were the stages that I watched human behavior play out on and I learned the nature of our nature. I began to create my own survival strategies to stay out of an alcoholic relationship, not engage in codependency, and maintain full custody of our child. My goal was to not be a crazy codependent and to not raise her in an alcoholic home nor a codependently sick home. This meant that I had to respectfully learn from others who learned these hard lessons the hard way. This was a key strategy. I also worked my hardest (a battle within) to avoid war and attacking the other party with court because it created more war. Accepting losses, maintaining my priority to my child, and marching on was how I won the war after losing some battles. Money wasn't worth it. Being right wasn't worth it. Our freedom was.

So, I said to myself, "Be respectful and learn from others!"

## My Take-a-way Strategy: Respectfully Learn From Others

I respectfully learned from others. I listened and learned to the many messy stories involving alcohol and codependent behaviors at meetings. I got some help. I gained some wisdom. I avoided more cost. I saved myself some money. I save our future.

❖ If you would like to read some of my other survival strategies and read FREE excerpts of my other books, please visit my website at: www.GraceWroldson.com

# Strategy #9:
# Tirelessly Teach Yourself

and

✓ Help Yourself
✓ Be Self-Taught,
✓ Do Self-Help
✓ Find and Follow

### Your Inner Teacher—Your Instincts

*"What we teach ourselves with our thoughts and attitudes is up to us."*
*— Al-Anon, In All Our Affairs*

**I often asked myself, "How do I teach myself when I don't have all the answers?"**

## What I Taught Myself in Life School

I looked for answers everywhere to help me with the overwhelming, all-consuming problem in my life: my relationship with the alcoholic. Life and that relationship was my classroom. I read countless books, countless times. I listened to experts, I attended AA meetings, and I joined Al-Anon. I even sought out several different spiritual paths, so I could privately speak with mentors, leaders, preachers, and teachers about this perplexing problem. **After twenty years of my research, I concluded that no *one* person, organization, or teaching had *all* the answers for my life. I had to learn to teach myself with what I knew and discovered from my own failed attempts at changing myself and loving an alcoholic.** I began to listen to myself and hear my own words of wisdom. I became self-taught on my own subjects of Me and My Life. I had to stop wondering what others would tell me to do, and stop to ask myself, "What would I tell me to do?" I discovered that I had some answers when I stopped and consulted my soul.

*"If you are willing to be a self-learner, you will develop yourself."*
— Lailah Gifty Akita, *Pearls of Wisdom: Great mind*

## Other People's Schools of Thought

As a student who often made mistakes, it was hard to hear some of the lectures in Life School, but I still needed an education and the lecture hall. A program friend of mine told me that the alcoholic was the key to my healing - that he was a messenger and his purpose was to show me my wounds. She insisted on her belief system, that at a very deep level, the alcoholic was a match to what was missing inside of me. I hated hearing that, especially after seven years free of the unsatisfying, turbulent, painful relationship. Having someone tell me that the alcoholic was still the key to healing myself and reaching a state of wholeness was infuriating. I didn't want to look at the alcoholic anymore. I didn't want to sit in his class. I didn't want to look deeper into the mess we made for inspiration to mature, move on, and grow. I was tired of all the drama he presented and all my reactions to his maneuvers. I just wanted to be free of him, his disease, and his disorders. I often walked out of her class biting my lip.

## Open To Learning New Ideas, Hearing The Truth

Processing this new idea, I found out that there was a certain knowing that I had inside of me. So when a teacher, friend, or mentor said something that rang true for me, I could actually feel a palpable lift and a resounding resonation inside of me. I began to catch those instances when I identified with the truth in this way. It became my signal to listen to what they were saying (even if I didn't like what I was hearing). Sometimes my soul and an Inner Knowing would pick up on these truths through what others were saying when they were attempting to advise me. But sometimes my Inner Knowing knew that

112

when they thought they were talking to me, about me, they were really speaking about themselves. Sometimes teachers like to rant.

*"Anybody who listens to their intuition risks at times making other people disappointed or even pissed off because you're not tending to what they want from you but instead to what feels right for you."*
— *Maria Erving*

## Feeling The Truth

What I discovered was that the truth felt awesome to hear and feel inside my body. However, I noted that 99% of what others advised was nothing I could work with at the time. But being the smart woman that I was, I stored the data, wisdom, and logic for later. I couldn't unhear what I had heard, so I kept their book on my shelf. Before maturing in my recovery programs, I did not have the inner resources to inwardly and emotionally navigate life (healthily); so I often needed the teachings and wisdom of others. I was very resourceful, as survivors are, and I found the libraries - so to speak.

*"It shouldn't matter what I say, but rather, how you feel—don't listen to the words of people. Instead, listen to your heart. It doesn't lie, and it is speaking just as loudly."*
— *Courtney Praski, The Seven*

## Starting A Self-Education

The first part of my recovery had to be about getting the education and finding the right teachers. However, I mistakenly thought that by attending Al-Anon, I was in a class that had found all the answers for my dilemma. At first, without any recovery education, I did have to sit as a student and get myself educated on the general "truths" that exist surrounding addiction. But there came a point for me (on about my eighteenth year) when I had too much dependence on what I thought was the school system. I was seeking answers from outside of myself rather than answers from inside myself. While I realized I would never "graduate" from the recovery program (because there is no graduation), I still benefited tremendously by staying in Al-Anon. Yet, I knew that I at least needed to graduate to the next level.

**My Lesson:**

✓  Teach Myself,
✓  Be Self-Taught

## Finding and Following My Inner Teacher

I needed to learn the lesson that, at times, I was my own best teacher. So, what did I want to teach myself? I strategized like any new graduate and asked my inner entrepreneur for a different way through the mess of co-parenting with an alcoholic and the continual court process of custody battles. Only I knew all the facts, tricks, sticking points, details, and past drama that played into my case. When there was a court related problem involving the alcoholic, I noticed that I would pick up the phone and call everyone I knew who was older, smarter, and had more years in recovery - to get some guidance. I noticed that I skipped over my own intuitive "hits" and "hints." I asked for help and advice hoping someone had the right ideas and right answers for me. I mistakenly thought that others had the answers for my life. This was yet another subtle way I was harming myself with people, as my codependent self often did. I had a whole classroom inside of me looking up at the messy chalkboard of my life. I didn't have the answers at first, but I had learned some valuable lessons and I felt like I had a degree (surviving 15 years in an alcoholic relationship) that I could use. My degree was an associate's degree in "The Study of Me." Personal recovery was my form of self-study and I was working towards my bachelor's.

## Self-Control, To Self-Esteem, To Instincts

It took a while to be able to hear my own internal answers. Struggling with codependency meant that I often ignored myself. As a codependent, I would skip over my own guidance (from my intuition) and do the next distracting thing. This, I had to watch out for by often asking myself, "What am I doing and why?" Automatic behavior led to a lot of worry, anxiety, and more piled-up problems. I exercised very little self-control with stopping myself from behaving this way (the way I had previously coped). With recovery, I discovered that self-control led to freedom. Self-control actually led to a direct path to solid self-esteem and surefootedness. So, I began to practice a gentle form of self-control and self-discipline in all areas of my life. What I noticed with recovery and a solid focus on myself was... that my instincts gradually came back.

## My Instincts

With years of recovery under my belt, my instincts for survival and leading a healthy life had more guidance and principles attached. My instincts now had backup, and I began to know why I felt certain things. I had taken the time to get to know myself through the process of recovery. I began to partner with myself rather than push myself away. I stopped myself from grabbing onto other people and instead grabbed a pen and paper. My rebuild began with what I started teaching myself.

*"As soon as you trust yourself, you will know how to live."*
— *Sally Brampton, Shoot the Damn Dog: A Memoir of Depression*

Throughout my struggles with codependency, something inside of me was always trying to reach me. I discovered my Inner Teacher. I began to learn life's series of lessons using an Inner Textbook. I sat at my own desk and read my own cliff notes. I began to teach myself with the lessons that I was learning. I started to use other people's help for brainstorming sessions and as a way to bounce ideas off of them - much like the reference section in the library - instead of relying on others to give me all the answers (which they didn't have anyway).

## I Love an Alcoholic, but Hated The Drinking

In my journals, I read messages from myself that were apologies to my soul for the lack of self-reliance and so much self-doubt. Some of those early, pre-recovery letters to myself confessed that I had betrayed myself. Because I had led myself down a path of learning that was extremely difficult. I lost a lot on alcoholic love. At those moments, I made vows to myself to be a person who supports herself —by listening to my intuition. I vowed to listen to myself and teach myself whatever I could. It was then that my rebuild and re-education really began. I started giving myself my own advice, based on my own circumstances because only I knew how to navigate them. The alcoholic wasn't done drinking, and unfortunately, I wasn't done having to deal with him. I didn't get deliverance from the alcoholic-codependent problem. I didn't get an easy way out of the trauma associated with loving an alcoholic codependently. I had to work through this disaster because no shortcut could work around it. So, I had to start teaching myself. And what was I teaching myself? I was teaching myself to trust myself. So, did I really have the answers I needed all along, somewhere inside of me? Yes, after some initial education and help. Finally, after years of asking others what they thought, I learned to ask myself, "What do I think?"

*"Trust yourself. Create the kind of self that you will be happy to live with all your life."*
*— Golda Meir*

## My Take-a-way Strategy: Tirelessly Teach Yourself

I tirelessly taught myself what I needed to know. I kept on learning about the effects of alcohol and being affected by alcoholism. I helped myself. I became self-taught and did self-help in Life School. I found and followed my Inner Teacher and came to know my instincts.

❖ If you would like to read some of my other survival strategies and read FREE excerpts of my other books, please visit my website at: www.GraceWroldson.com

116

# Strategy #10:
# Mindfully Hear Your Own Words,

✓ Then Listen to Yourself
✓ Your Words, Your Wisdom
✓ Choose New Words

*"A broken bone can heal, but the wound a word opens can fester forever."*
*—Jessamyn West*

**I asked myself, "Who was I going to listen to: myself or the alcoholic?"**

## The Garden of My Mind

His words held power. I could still hear the alcoholic's words in my head almost a decade later. A counselor that I was seeing weekly told me that one of the last things to leave you from an abusive relationship are the hurtful words that were used as weapons. Unfortunately, these recordings played over and over in my mind (between my ears) as if they were being heard again and again. Even though I had broken up with him and shut him out, I still had to find the switch to shut him off!

Getting into a relationship with an alcoholic who liked to talk set me up for being the listener. When he said things that I wanted to hear, I hung onto his words and let him spill, spell, and speak. In the early years of the relationship, I loved his words. I was hypnotized by his promises as they seemed to cast a spell over my codependent, small self. As I recovered and learned my lessons, I had to learn to love *my* words - said to me. This is how I broke the spell.

I Love an Alcoholic, but Hated The Drinking

**Words Have Power**

**What I didn't realize was that words have tremendous power—enough to last years and lifetimes. I also didn't know my own words equally held great power —when I dared to speak.** I courageously began to choose my words over his. Speaking one-on-one weekly (sometimes daily) with my trusted sponsor, I cultivated my voice and learned to articulate and internalize my own vocabulary. I fertilized with phone calls. **I discovered that I had the ability to talk back to the alcoholic's purposefully planted words that grew like unwanted weeds in my mind.** His words were indeed just like seeds planted (in me) for eventual sowing. So, I learned to become a constant gardener.

I was learning the power of my own words because the alcoholic's words had proven very powerful. Words had the ability to possess me. When I caught onto how each word spoken represented something symbolically, I began to tap into that earth and speak the words that I most needed to hear. I grew those words within me, until they were tall and strong. I said and wrote things to myself in my journal that I needed to hear (from myself) like, "I am safe and supported." **My words became my power.** My words became my medicine and I needed daily doses of myself. Raised in my family not to speak, I had never developed the muscles to speak up for myself, so I didn't have the words at first. I had to mull things over in my mind (and find the right words for me) so I didn't get mowed over by the alcoholic.

**My Lesson:**

✓ Hear my own words,
✓ then listen to myself.

**My Words, My Wisdom**

I learned that what mattered to me were my words and my wisdom. Having survived a drought of self-love that lasted half my lifetime (and the whole alcoholic relationship), I owned that my wisdom had grown. My wisdom now took first place in this garden of my mind, not his words. My new principle (and focus) had to be listening to myself, and this had to extend out to everyone who spoke to me, not just the alcoholic. I had to learn to not give power to other people's negative words directed at me by believing them. I had to believe myself.

## My Words Were Right For Me

I found out that no one had the right words for what I was trying to say to myself. I had to come up with the script and develop the words that were right for me. When I started writing my first book, I found it amazing how changing one little word could change the entire meaning of what I was actually trying to say. Freelance writers who helped me edit my lessons were trying to make my writing grammatically correct, yet I was trying to be truthful grammatically. They would suggest other formatting to make things fit the "proper" sentence structure, yet I was formatting the lessons to make them fit my truth. I had to completely ignore some of their expert suggestions because it didn't fit my situation. I found it dangerous to allow them to change words I didn't approve of because some of the changes made me sound like a victim who blamed the alcoholic versus me having and holding my power, and taking responsibility for myself. I began to sit back and see that the well-intentioned freelancers only saw the surface of what should be said in my situation. But I no longer lived on "shoulds" and surfaces, I had my roots in recovery.

## I Can Grow

Having to read edits that didn't match my recovery reminded me of what my old life (in the alcoholic relationship) looked like to other people. In that old life, I was living a lie, appearing to be in a loving relationship with the alcoholic. Everything on the outside, everything that other people saw, seemed perfect because there was no visible

I Love an Alcoholic, but Hated The Drinking

conflict or fighting. My codependency covered everything up that it could, until it couldn't. If I were to have told people what life was really like they would have thought I was the liar and not that the relationship lived on a lie. If I wrote a behind the scenes true story for everyone in my old circle of friends, it would not have made sense to any reader who "knew" us. The sculpted bushes and the manicured lawn around our relationship fooled everyone who drove by. The only one who knew what was happening was me. The only one who knew me was me, and I was learning every day that I could grow and change. I had a secret garden.

## Choose New Words

What did I want to say to myself? What did I need to say to myself? I had to consciously choose new words. I used the words of a victor and not that of a victim because I couldn't be powerful and pitiful at the same time. Believing the alcoholic's words were, in reality, like watering them. So, I began repeating my own words which watered the new beliefs that I wanted to be part of my new/next life. I removed words like *fault, blame*, and *deserve* from my vocabulary. I opted for a different kind of speech when telling my story.

What were my new words? They consisted of *recovery, responsibility,* and *freedom*. My self-talk became an asset and an ally rather than an internal enemy. The alcoholic was no longer around talking at me. I was there, having a monologue with myself. So, I chose to master it. I chose new words. I asked myself, "What is it I most need to hear?" (and I reiterated that to myself on a daily basis). I learned to tell myself, "You are important." "Your voice matters." "Your words, your wisdom."

*"When we speak we are afraid our words will not be heard or welcomed. But when we are silent, we are still afraid. So it is better to speak."*
— *Audre Lorde*

## My Take-a-way Strategy: Mindfully Hear My Own Words Then Listen to Myself

I mindfully heard my own words of wisdom and began listening to myself. I choose new words to create the new life I wanted to be living. I replanted the garden of my mind with good thoughts.

❖ If you would like to read some of my other survival strategies and read FREE excerpts of my other books, please visit my website at: www.GraceWroldson.com

# Strategy #11:
# Ferociously Take a Strong Strength-Based Approach

    ✓  Pass the "Tests"
   ✓  Developing a Backbone
   ✓  See Yourself Differently

*"The first gift is Strength. May you remember to call upon it whenever you need it."*
— *Charlene Costanzo,* The Twelve Gifts of Birth

**I asked myself, "Am I weak or am I strong?"**

## *Standing and Sitting Up Straight*

I had a spiritual experience. It felt more like a truth-straightening experience. Sitting on my new counselor's red couch, I sat up straighter and taller as my shift happened. It felt like all my weakness had been lifted up and that she, my counselor, had built a base for this strength. In my past years of therapy, I was seeing myself from a very skewed perception after feeling victimized in an alcoholic relationship. If a spiritual path is the path of Truth, then I had a spiritual experience at my first counseling session with a domestic violence counselor because I was getting an adjustment to the Truth. Before this first session, I had never asked myself if I was in an abusive relationship. I was only asking myself if the alcoholic (or living with alcoholism) was the right choice for me. The answer to the second question was no, but, to the first question, the answer was yes. I found my strength when I took a strong, strength-based approach for myself— with my new counselor.

    I walked into her new office slouched over, I had come from three years of working with a private, licensed therapist who specialized in adult-child issues. I had thought that she was (and had to be) the best fit for my alcoholic dilemma. However, after three years, I felt like I had blamed myself for my life and all the problems with the alcoholic. I slumped on her brown couch, sank into it, and sometimes curled up in fear, blame, and shame on it. Taking responsibility for being in that relationship had bogged me down into thinking that I was totally defective. Feeling more flawed, I wanted something different from my weekly sessions. I wanted personal empowerment to overcome the alcoholic-codependent dilemma. I didn't know that it was disempowering for me to constantly find fault with myself and continuously pick my mind and behavior apart in therapy. Who was I if I was just finding all my faults? (This was actually another adult-child issue of mine.) It didn't build me up, it down-right weakened me. I never stopped to ask myself if was she the right therapist for me (or her approach), at least not until I met my new counselor.

*"Go within every day and find the inner strength so that the world will not blow your candle out."* — *Katherine Dunham*

## A New Set of Eyes With Which To See Myself

Feeling defective, I started craving a life coach, spiritual director, or something else instead. I was craving the Truth. It took me a whole year to get the courage to seek a different form of help. I found free therapy for women in tough situations at a local domestic violence office and I decided to give something different a try. So, there I was, a scared woman, sitting on her red, velvet couch in her office with a Zen sandbox, a Buddha statue with rocks and crystals sprinkled here and there. I gave her a brief summary of my situation feeling like an idiot to have gotten myself into so much of a mess and needing so much help. I was surprised when she looked at me puzzled. So, I finally gave her a turn to speak. She said that she saw me as a strong, educated, resourceful, and resilient woman. Huh!? Oh…! Impressed, I sat up straighter and taller with each new adjective she used to describe me. It's like my spine snapped into place with every word of strength she saw in me. It was after that first session with her that I learned I needed empowerment to get me through. I needed someone who saw me as whole and capable. She was seeing me completely differently than I had been seeing myself by working with an adult-child therapist. She saw the strength in my story, and that made me sit up.

## Seeing Myself Differently

I asked myself, "Who was I becoming? and, "Who did I want to be?" Going to a new counselor helped me to see myself differently. I saw that, despite the many defects of character I had when I was in an alcoholic relationship (which I had openly confessed to my first therapist), I did have good character assets. To get over the last hump of healing from the toxic relationship, I needed to see myself as strong and capable. I had survived the relationship, and now I needed to stay strong and grow even stronger. I was a mother with a mission. I knew that the old, outdated idea— that getting help was a sign of weakness— was no longer society's judgment. Getting help was now *a sign of strength*. So, being strong, I got help. I had a team to help me in my early recovery that included a sponsor, mentor, spiritual director, program friends (with thirty years of recovery/program experience), and a counselor. I had a strong team, and their support strengthened me.

*"The best advice I can give to anyone going through a rough patch is to never be afraid to ask for help."*
*— Demi Lovato, Stay Strong*

## Getting Past Self-Pity to Self-Esteem

Before this "red couch experience," feeling sorry for myself led to chronic self-pity. Former friends who believed that self-pity was love, loved me from that place. But only the people who saw me as a capable woman could help me build my strength. I was sitting down in self-pity when I needed to be standing up straight —with a strong sense of self.

## Stopping Myself From Sourcing From Others

My experience of the contrast between therapy approaches taught me that I needed to stop sourcing from others and partner with myself. I needed to consult my inner-self and my soul with what to do in certain sticky situations. **I realized that it was dangerous (for me) to stay in a relationship (even in a patient-therapy relationship) for too long because I would become dependent on how the other person viewed me and become dependent on their inner resources —instead of self-sourcing my own.** This was another codependency issue of mine— arising when I was sitting in front of another person, allowing myself to be judged, and taking their perspective of me as the ultimate truth. By looking for outer approval from just one person and putting a therapist on a pedestal, it showed me that I hadn't built a solid sense of self yet. Being able to respectfully end therapy with the adult-child therapist and move on for myself was like passing a personal "test" of being able to do what I need to do— even if someone else didn't like it.

*"I was always looking outside myself for strength and confidence, but it comes from within. It is there all the time."*
*— Anna Freud*

Looking back, I know that the three years that I dedicated to therapy, dealing with my ACOA issues, was still good for me in many, many ways. The time spent owning my "stuff" was necessary for me to take responsibility for myself and come up higher. It was part of my healing processes. So, in a way… therapy worked!

## Restore Lost Power, Making A List

I also needed to list the "tests" in life that I had already passed using my recovery in Al-Anon and a Higher Power. Often, I felt that Life gave me challenges to overcome by using my recovery (or not). I often felt like a Higher Power was with me and encouraging me to keep standing. I knew my soul saw everything. My "tests" came in various forms of small daily challenges, as well as bigger life decisions on letting go of relationships that no longer served me. Some of these "tests" were serious. With solid recovery, and a higher perspective on life, I was surprised that I could now identify if I was choosing life or death, with any given problem. Tests were everywhere. When I was met with what I considered a test, I asked myself this most important question, "What's being asked of me right now?", "Will this choice be a choice that chooses life?"

## Remembering My Ability To Heal With Lists

One year, when I was sick and recovering from several surgeries and wondering if my body could heal and repair, a wise doctor told me to list all the surgeries and injuries I had overcome in the past in order to see that I was capable of healing again. When I listed all that I had survived and read back over it, I could see my healing abilities (strengths). I had to list the things that I *had* overcome and *had* already healed from to remember all the positive traits about me. I needed to remember all of my innate abilities that alcoholism hadn't taken away and that my codependency hadn't given away. I felt taller when I walked with the inner-knowledge that I had passed certain "tests" and that I did indeed have the power to heal. Creating lists somehow strengthened me. So, I made lists, and that became my strength-based approach to becoming stronger.

## Finding My Back-Bone

As a codependent, I was often soft-boned. I felt that my sensitivity and sweetness was a gift. I never tried to be harder and tougher. I learned that while it was a gift to be an empath, loving, caring, and nice... it didn't help me walk strongly into a sometimes harsh world. I was thin-skinned, and in childhood I was often told to "toughen up." Things bothered my conscious easily. Also before recovery, other people's energy could get "in" because my boundaries were weak. With recovery, however, I had attended enough meetings to know a few things that I believed to be true —and that helped me stand up for myself. My program gave me a solid foundation that I could always return to. When life would happen, when I was challenged, when "tests" came up, I could go to a meeting for strength and then apply my program. The program became a solid foundation for me. Meetings were everywhere and every day. I attended meetings to keep my strength and stay strong. Every meeting built my backbone of knowledge. And knowledge contained some power for me. The people in the program became my recovery friends. And, at first, I relied on their backbones and their bravery to build my own base. They couldn't do it for me.

*"I found an inner strength to fight for myself. It was clear that nobody else would."*
— *Tehmina Durrani, My Feudal Lord*

From a place of empowerment, I took a strength-based approach to everything in my life. I made my recovery, program tools, and meetings the solid foundation that I could go back to with every issue - not just when I faced issues concerning the alcoholic. **What I didn't realize at first was that the program wasn't for the alcoholic, it was for me.** Now, I was working recovery to have a better relationship with myself and not the alcoholic. I began to benefit from the meetings in every way since I was there for me. So, when I felt weak, I asked myself, "What are my strengths?" When I felt broken, I asked myself, "What have I already overcome and healed from?" When I felt lost, I asked myself, "When and where is the next and nearest meeting?" or "What does my Higher Power have to say about where I am?" When I was at any difficult point in life with myself, I didn't ask my new counselor, I remembered to ask, "What's being asked of me right now?" And I dared to ask myself, "How strong can I be about this?"

*"Strength does not come from physical capacity. It comes from an indomitable will."*

Grace W. Wroldson
— *Mahatma Gandhi*

## My Take-a-way Strategy: Ferociously Take a Strong Strength-Based Approach

I ferociously took a strong strength-based approach. I passed the tests and developed a backbone. I began to see myself as strong, capable, and able. I stood up tall and sat up straight. I stood for myself and was able to stand all by myself with my new found strength.

❖ If you would like to read some of my other survival strategies and read FREE excerpts of my other books, please visit my website at: www.GraceWroldson.com

# Discovering My Choices

*Once I came to realize that I have a choice and that the choice is mine...*

I choose to live by choice, not chance.
I choose to focus on me, not you.
I choose to make changes, not excuses.
I choose to be motivated, not manipulated.
I choose self-esteem, not self-pity.
I choose to be filled with hope, not despair.
I choose to excel, not compete.
I choose *my* life, not yours.

I choose to focus on the good, not the bad.
I choose to walk with love, not with fear.
I choose to keep the faith, not to doubt.
I choose to find me, not you.

I choose to forgive, not forget.
I choose to be a victor, not a victim.
I choose to stand up, not stand still.
I choose to be in the present,
not in the past.
I choose to move forward, not backward.
I choose to bless, not to curse.
I choose freedom, not chains.

I choose to surrender, not to control.
I choose to guide me, not try to guide you.
I choose self-assurance, not self-doubt.
I choose to live in truth, not surrounded by lies.
I choose inner peace, not inner anger.

Grace W. Wroldson

I choose to thrive, not merely settle to survive.
I choose to save myself, not abandon you.

I choose to walk my own journey, not walk yours.
I choose to live by wisdom, not by woe.
I choose to listen to me, not to you.

I choose to transform my pain, not hold on to it.
I choose to transcend my negativity, not release it on you.
I choose to care for me, and for you.
I choose to feel sympathy for myself, compassion for you.
I choose to be true to myself, rather than you.

I choose to live in joy, not in pain.
I choose to make God my Higher Power, not you.
I choose what really matters.

There are choices to be made.
I choose to give myself the gift of choice.

I choose a life of choice.


— *Grace W. Wroldson*

# My Gift to You

**(My 2 Bonus Strategies)**

**Strategy #12:**
**It's All About Choices**

**&**

**Strategy #13:**
**It's All About Love**

*"You need to go from wanting to change your life to deciding to change your life. If you want to live a life you've never lived, you've to do things you've never done."*
— *Jen Sincero, You Are a Badass : How to Stop Doubting Your Greatness and Start Living an Awesome Life*

# Strategy #12:
# Consciously Choose Everything

✓ Make New Choices,
✓ Choices Have Consequences

✓ Choose new words

**The Power of Choices**

*"You may not be able to choose different circumstances. But you can choose to thrive in every circumstance."*
— *Tama Kieves, Thriving Through UnCertainty*

**I asked myself, "Can I choose my way out of the alcoholic relationship disaster?"**

## *Having Choices,*
## *Choosing Differently*

Seven years after an alcoholic relationship, I realized that I was a victim of my own choices. I had choices available to me that I didn't know I had. Now, I discovered that I had choices in what I chose to think about the alcoholic dilemma. To heal, I had to undergo phases of corrective thinking. It was like a business plan I was establishing with my brain, in my brain. When I chose new thoughts, new feelings were generated as a byproduct. The end results of choosing new thoughts was the successful output of feelings such as; hope, possibility, gratitude. I had a mental factory that needed a solid business plan based on blessings— and seeing blessings. My brain was always so busy doing what brains do. It often worked unpaid, in overtime, on burn-out mode.

**I made a plan to choose differently and do business differently because what was being created was not a healthy, happy, content life.** So, I chose my way out of the alcoholic relationship. Choice by choice. I chose my way into a new and better life for myself and my child with a solid plan. Choice by choice. I created a new better "business of living" plan. I did not give up. I allowed myself to ache deep down but I did not allow myself to go down. I let appearances crumble. But I did not give up on myself. I had the tremendous capacity to reinvent myself —we all do. I died to who I used to be but I did not die to who I really was. It was a start-up of a new life. This business plan was personal.

*"Freedom is what you do with what's been done to you."*
— *Jean-Paul Sartre*

## Choice is My Power

My sponsor told me that I had choices when it came to my reactions. I wondered, was a reaction just a choice I was making? When I was so easily reactive to the alcoholic and our stressful court situation, I couldn't see my reactions as a choice. My sponsor told me I could choose to be triggered or not. In my triggered state, I could not see that choice available - at all. Reacting and triggers seemed to take over my entire being and I would be launched into fear, anxiety, and harmful amounts of worrying. In my circuitry, in my mental factory, I could not find the wire to cut to stop reacting. It seemed so natural because it was my naturally practiced state. I couldn't find the place inside me that needed healing to stop setting myself up for triggers. Being triggered felt like a permanent problem I would have the rest of my life even though I was practicing all other good recovery behaviors such as picking up the phone and talking to a program friend when I was in these terrible states.

That was until I created a new business plan. A good business plan takes into account the future as well as the past. I had to utilize my resources from my years of recovery as well as seek out new resources.

134

I needed strategies that moved past my old survival programs. I needed strategies that involved choice. Choice became my power when I felt like I lost all power. I chose not to react. I chose to remain calm. I did this by staying consciously aware of my feelings and inner state. Instead of running away from all my fears, I turned to face them with the Steps of the program and they lost power. I had no idea that running away gave my fears power. I took my power back.

*"You are very powerful, provided you know how powerful you are. "*
*— Yogi Bhajan*

My new business plan was how I was going to go about the business of living my life. This meant daily business meetings. I had to remain conscious about my choices. I had to start noticing my fearful reactive states and talk myself down from them (and call in a consultant). This meant that I needed to practice being mindful and have a team, as well as, be on my own team. I was mindful of what I was doing, how much of it, and who I was doing it with. Because everything mattered. Every choice had a consequence. So I made good, solid, mature choices; and I experienced better consequences. I had a new business model that allowed me to enjoy my life, whether the alcoholic was drinking or not.

*"Remember always that you not only have the right to be an individual, you have an obligation to be one."*
*— Eleanor Roosevelt*

I was brought up under the pretense that if someone or something could change, then my life could change and become more fulfilling. I was waiting for the alcoholic to change but it was taking him years and decades (and it didn't happen). I lost hope. Thankfully, I lost hope in that type of conditional living. **I put my new hope in myself about what *I* could do if *I* changed.** I chose to catch my mental breath and examine my thought factory and warehouse. What was I telling myself about my life that was so upsetting? Could I tell myself something different? I made choices in which thoughts I chose to think. I learned to love myself with choices.

## Loving Myself with Choices

I chose not to be in an alcoholic relationship continuing my pattern of codependency. In spite of my sorrows, I learned to live with a broken heart and learn how to make my heart happy. I healed, I changed, and I transformed. I loved having new choices to choose from. Becoming conscious (of myself and situation with the alcoholic) was my full-time curriculum from the Universe. Staying conscious was my new full-time job.

*"The only person who can pull me down is myself, and I'm not going to let myself pull me down anymore."*
— *C. JoyBell C.*

## I chose:

- I choose to be courageous and confess my codependent behaviors to myself and my sponsor. (This kept me accountable.)
- I chose to fearlessly focus on myself and my healing journey—not the alcoholic.
- I chose to tenaciously learn my life lessons and keep learning.
- I chose to steadfastly stay spiritual and have a higher power.
- I chose to be audacious and question everything, especially my motives.
- I chose to aggressively pinpoint my patterns and intercept unhealthy ones as well as, create healthy ones.
- I chose to respectfully learn from others and listen to their wisdom.

- I chose to tirelessly teach myself and continue to grow and evolve.
- I chose to practice mindfulness and change the vocabulary I was using.
- I chose to ferociously take a strong strength-based approach to my life and living.
- I chose to consciously choose everything and make new choices.
- I chose to passionately practice self-love.

So, I said to myself, "Be conscious when making choices!"

*"What lies behind us and what lies before us are tiny matters compared to what lies within us."* — *Ralph Waldo Emerson*

## My Take-a-way Strategy: Consciously Choose Everything

I consciously began to choose everything and make new choices. I found that my choices have consequences, so I needed to stay conscious at all times. I looked for where I had choices. I discovered my choices. I loved myself with better choices.

❖ If you would like to read some of my other survival strategies and read FREE excerpts of my other books, please visit my website at: www.GraceWroldson.com

# Strategy #13:
# Passionately Practice Self-Love

✓  Learn To Turn Your Love Upon Yourself!
*(and your children - if you have any)*
✓  Love Yourself The Way A Higher Power Would Love You

*"The most enlightened prayer isn't "Dear God, send me someone wonderful," but*
*"Dear God, help me realize that I am someone wonderful."*
— *Marianne Williamson, A Return To Love*

**I asked myself, "If I was that passionate about loving an alcoholic, could I be as passionate about loving myself?"**

## *Loving the Rewards of Self-Love*

I loved the alcoholic so much that I didn't even notice when I had stopped loving myself. I was deprived of love. When I realized that I was depriving myself (and stopped blaming the alcoholic), I quit trying to love the alcoholic back into health and happiness. Instead, I tried to love myself with that same passion. I turned all of my outward loving of him, inward (at me), where it was needed the most. I desperately needed my own love.

*"Becoming acquainted with yourself is a price well worth paying*
*for the love that will really address your needs."*
— *Daphne Rose Kingma*

### Loving Acts

At first, I found practicing self-love to be a real challenge. However, with time and effort this became a new skill. It took years of practice and patience with myself. First, I had to define self-love. In the beginning I could only work with love as a verb and do self-loving acts. Seeing love in action helped me understand what self-love looked like practiced. Then the self-love solution and "self-love skill" turned into a healthy habit that developed. My new loving actions had new lovely outcomes. **Now, I reap the rewards of self-love daily.**

*"If you aren't good at loving yourself, you will have a difficult time loving anyone, since you'll resent the time and energy you give another person that you aren't even giving to yourself."*
— *Barbara De Angelis*

## Love Is The Answer

Love was the answer. I wasn't able to get healthy love from the alcoholic, so I had to get the love from myself. **My self-help solution was self-love.** Self-love was my secret weapon (in my war within). I just plain and simple loved myself back to life. I loved myself back to health and wholeness. I couldn't hate myself into health. It didn't work. I also couldn't hate the alcoholic and get healthy. That didn't work, either. Instead of all that hate, I loved myself the way I believe my Higher Power loves me. Self-love was the right kind of love for me. I found that love— in the right form, applied the in the right way, to the right person (me), had the most healing power of all.

❖ For me, self-love started with self-respect. I began by respecting myself.

*"Plant your own garden and decorate your own soul, instead of waiting for someone to bring you flowers."*
— *Veronica A. Shoffstall*

I love hearing from readers on how they helped themselves by creating their own creative strategies for surviving their situations, as well as, surviving their codependency. Please visit: www.GraceWroldson.com for more FREE strategies.

*"If you can love a person so much that you travel to the depths of hell, imagine how amazing you could be at loving yourself?"*
— *Grace W. Wroldson*

# Tears of Gratitude

*I would cry*

First...
My tears were of pain,
My tears were of sorrow,

My tears were of loss,
My tears were of pity,

My tears were of past depressions,
My tears were of future fears,

My tears were for him,
My tears were for me,

When I finally understood...
My tears emerged like new green grass in the Spring
My tears stopped like a hard Summer rain when I accepted
My tears flowed into rivers of compassion
and fell like Autumn leaves into beautiful colors on Earth's floor
My tears froze like beautiful crystals of Winter ice
during the holidays.

Then...
My tears sprung up
and signaled of my growth
My tears pushed through personal breakthroughs
My tears poured from my heart when I dance with joy
My tears answered happy memories that resurfaced when I reminisced
My tears broke through the heaviness with bursts of laughter
My tears glistened when I savored my serenity

My tears were part of the seasons of my life
My tears were of gratitude

I still cry

— *Grace W. Wroldson*

# *My Promises*

- ❖ As I practice recovery, my recovery will make my life better.
- ❖ I will treat myself with kindness because kindness matters.
- ❖ As I practice personal integrity, I heal and honor my soul.
- ❖ I will practice loyalty to myself and remain loyal.
- ❖ As I develop trust with myself, I will grow to always trust myself.
- ❖ I will believe in myself, even if nobody else does.
- ❖ As I keep my commitments to myself, I bless my life and future.
- ❖ I will feel safe and secure within myself as I choose to self-partner, self-source, and self-protect.
- ❖ As I keep my past codependency issues in mind, I create a new relationship with myself.
- ❖ I will be gentle with myself when I make mistakes.
- ❖ As I stay sober from all my addictions to loving others, I can then love myself.
- ❖ I will thank my inner guidance for fear and consider my fears as loving messages to take into serious consideration.
- ❖ I will care for myself and about myself.
- ❖ As I allow my Higher Power to change me for the better, I will enjoy the new version of me that emerges.
- ❖ I will allow myself to feel my feelings.
- ❖ As I practice wholeness, my loneliness and despair will dissolve.
- ❖ I will practice self-preservation.
- ❖ Gradually, I will feel safe to speak up for myself and my beliefs, staying true to myself. And if I can't (for whatever legal/safety reason), I will speak with my own soul, sponsor, and my Higher Power about the truth.

- ❖ I will take a stand for myself, even several hundred stands if needed.
- ❖ As I work my program, I will make being conscious a full-time job.
- ❖ I will keep my eyes wide open as I walk through life.
- ❖ In complicated circumstances, I will do my best and not beat myself up for not knowing/doing better.
- ❖ I will remember that I am human and need compassion.
- ❖ As I learn more about myself, I will know myself better.
- ❖ I will build a solid sense of self and feel stable and supported with a strong inner identity.
- ❖ As I become more authentic, so will my life.
- ❖ I will maintain a focus on my recovery, myself, my life, my health, my finances, my career, my goals, my stability, and my child.
- ❖ I will choose in my best interest over other people's best interest.
- ❖ I will do what is right for me and my child in every situation.
- ❖ As I rely on a Higher Power, I will be given the strength that I need - on a daily basis.
- ❖ I will stay aware of my perfectionism issues, negative thinking, tendency to worry, anxious feelings, and work to think constructive, positive thoughts.
- ❖ Going forward, I will walk with self-confidence and cease chronic self-doubt.
- ❖ I will place my Higher Power everywhere in my life.
- ❖ With this, I will intuitively make healthier decisions, believing for a better, brighter future.
- ❖ I will then courageously place myself at the center of my own life.
- ❖ I will love myself the way God loves me.
- ❖ As I practice all these promises to myself, my happiness and joy will return.
- ❖ I will live with Love.

# *Additional Resources*

*So You Love an... Alcoholic?: Lessons for a Codependent.* by Grace W. Wroldson, Balboa: 2018

(available on Amazon)


Twelve-Step Family Group Resources:


Al-Anon Family Groups: Help and Hope for Families and Friends of Alcoholics, https://al-anon.org


*One Day at a Time in Al-Anon.* New York: Al-Anon Family Group Headquarter, 1974

*Courage to Change: One Day at a Time in Al-Anon II.* Al-Anon Family Group HQ, 1992


Other:

*Codependent No More: How to Stop Controlling Others and Start Caring for Yourself.*

by Melody Beattie: Hazelden- 1986, 1992


Website:

For more FREE strategies, please visit my website at www.GraceWroldson.com

Made in the USA
Middletown, DE
02 August 2022

70402025R00087